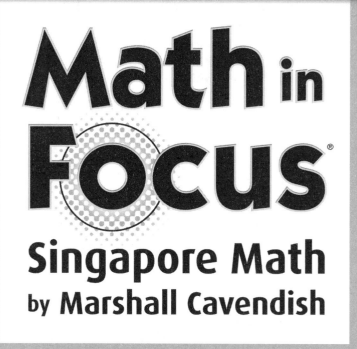

Math in Focus®

Singapore Math
by Marshall Cavendish

Activity Book

Author

Lois Chee
Voltaire Yap

Marshall Cavendish
Education

US Distributor

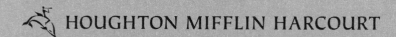
HOUGHTON MIFFLIN HARCOURT

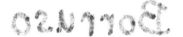

Published by Marshall Cavendish Education
An imprint of Marshall Cavendish International (Singapore) Private Limited
Times Centre, 1 New Industrial Road, Singapore 536196
Customer Service Hotline: (65) 6411 0820
E-mail: tmesales@sg.marshallcavendish.com
Website: www.marshallcavendish.com/education

Distributed by
Houghton Mifflin Harcourt
222 Berkeley Street
Boston, MA 02116
Tel: 617-351-5000
Website: www.hmheducation.com/mathinfocus

Cover: © Mike Hill/Getty Images

First published 2013

Math in Focus® Activity Book Course 3
ISBN 978-0-547-57898-9

Printed in United States of America

2 3 4 5 6 7 8   1401   17 16 15 14 13 12
4500358143   A B C D E

Contents

Introducing Math in Focus® Activity Book

The *Activity Book*, created to complement **Math in Focus®: Singapore Math by Marshall Cavendish**, provides additional projects and activities to deepen students' mathematical experiences. These projects and activities allow students to model mathematics, reason abstractly about new content, make sense of non-routine problems, and persevere in solving them.

Using the Activity Book

The *Activity Book* contains either a paper-and-pencil activity or a technology activity to accompany one lesson in each chapter of *Math in Focus®*. It also contains a project for each chapter that can be done either with a partner or a small group. Some activities and projects can be used as an alternate approach to what is taught in the Student Book, and others are extensions of what is in the Student Book. Each activity and project includes a scoring rubric, recording sheets and templates for students, and an answer key with solutions.

The *Activity Book* is also available online and on the Teacher One Stop CD-ROM.

1 Exponents

Lesson 1.2 Activity: Product and Quotient of Powers

Teacher's Guide

Type of activity	Hands-on activity
Objective	Reinforce the understanding of the product of powers rule.
Materials	• Patterns on pages 5 and 6 • Colored pencils or markers (optional)
Time	20–30 min
Ability levels	Mixed
Prerequisite skills	Understand and use exponential notation and prime factorization.
Grouping	Students should work alone or in pairs.
Assessment of students' learning	See Lesson 1.2 Activity: Rubric.
Preparation	Make sufficient copies of the patterns on pages 5 and 6 before the activity.

Lesson 1.2 Activity
Rubric

Category	4	3	2	1
Mathematical concepts	Explanation shows complete understanding of the mathematical concepts used to solve the problem(s).	Explanation shows substantial understanding of the mathematical concepts used to solve the problem(s).	Explanation shows some understanding of the mathematical concepts needed to solve the problem(s).	Explanation shows very limited understanding of the underlying concepts needed to solve the problem(s) OR is not written.
Self-assessment	Self-assessment is accurate and explanation is detailed and clear.	Self-assessment is fairly accurate and explanation is clear.	Self-assessment is inaccurate and explanation is a little difficult to understand, but includes critical components.	Self-assessment is totally inaccurate and explanation is difficult to understand and is missing several components OR is not included.
Working with others	Student was an engaged partner, listening to suggestions of others and working cooperatively throughout the lesson.	Student was an engaged partner but had trouble listening to others and/or working cooperatively.	Student cooperated with others, but needed prompting to stay on task.	Student did not work effectively with others.
Reflection	The reflection shows clear thought and effort. The learning experience being reflected upon is relevant to the student and learning goals.	The reflection shows a lot of thought and effort. Student makes attempts to demonstrate relevance, but the relevance is unclear in reference to learning goals.	The reflection shows some thought and effort. Some sections of the reflection are irrelevant to the student and/or learning goals.	The reflection is superficial. Most of the reflection is irrelevant to student and/or learning goals.

Lesson 1.2 Activity
Product and Quotient of Powers

Complete these steps for each pattern of polygons, using the chart on the Student Recording Sheet:

Step 1   Find the number of each type of polygon in the shaded part of each pattern.

Step 2   Find the number of times the shaded part of each pattern is repeated in each respective complete pattern on pages 5 and 6. You can use colored pencils to help keep track of the repeated shapes.

Step 3   Write the prime factorization of each of the numbers you found in Steps 1 and 2 in exponential notation.

Step 4   Use your prime factorizations from Step 3 to find the total number of each type of polygon in each complete pattern.

Step 5   Answer the questions on the Student Recording Sheet.

Name: _____   Date: _____

Lesson 1.2 Activity
Student Recording Sheet

Shaded Part of Pattern	Number of Octagons in Shaded Part of Pattern	Number of Squares in Shaded Part of Pattern	Number of Times Pattern is Repeated	Number of Octagons in Complete Pattern	Number of Squares in Complete Pattern

Shaded Part of Pattern	Number of Squares in Shaded Part of Pattern	Number of Equilateral Triangles in Shaded Part of Pattern	Number of Times Pattern is Repeated	Number of Squares in Complete Pattern	Number of Equilateral Triangles in Complete Pattern

Shaded Part of Pattern	Number of Squares in Shaded Part of Pattern	Number of Equilateral Triangles in Shaded Part of Pattern	Number of Times Pattern is Repeated	Number of Squares in Complete Pattern	Number of Equilateral Triangles in Complete Pattern

1. Which property did you use to find the total number of each type of polygon in the complete patterns?

2. When can you use this property?

Reflection

3. Describe what you learned about exponents from this activity.

© Marshall Cavendish International (Singapore) Private Limited.

Lesson 1.2 Activity
Materials

Complete pattern of octagons and squares

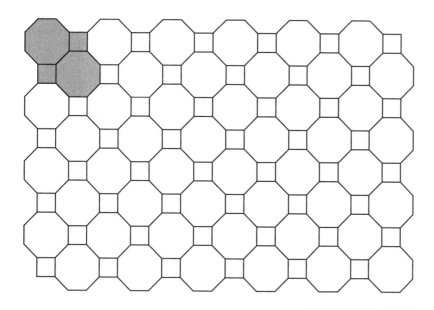

Lesson 1.2 Activity Continued
Materials

Complete pattern of squares and equilateral triangles

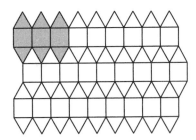

Complete pattern of squares and equilateral triangles

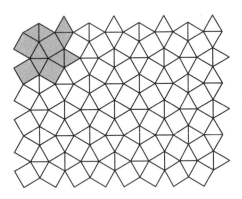

CHAPTER 1 Exponents

Project: Exponent Construction

Teacher's Guide

Common Core	
Common Core State Standard	8.EE1 Know and apply the properties of integer exponents to generate equivalent numerical expressions.
Objective	Reinforce the use of properties of exponents to simplify expressions.
Material	Calculator
Time	20–30 min
Ability levels	Mixed
Prerequisite skills	Understand the properties of exponents.
Grouping	Students should work in small groups.
Assessment of students' learning	See Chapter 1 Project: Rubric.

Chapter 1 Project
Rubric

Category	4	3	2	1
Mathematical concepts	Explanation shows complete understanding of the mathematical concepts used to solve the problem(s).	Explanation shows substantial understanding of the mathematical concepts used to solve the problem(s).	Explanation shows some understanding of the mathematical concepts needed to solve the problem(s).	Explanation shows very limited understanding of the underlying concepts needed to solve the problem(s) OR is not written.
Mathematical reasoning	Uses complex and refined mathematical reasoning.	Uses effective mathematical reasoning.	Shows some evidence of mathematical reasoning.	Shows little evidence of mathematical reasoning.
Working with others	Student was an engaged partner, listening to suggestions of others and working cooperatively throughout the lesson.	Student was an engaged partner but had trouble listening to others and/or working cooperatively.	Student cooperated with others, but needed prompting to stay on task.	Student did not work effectively with others.
Self-assessment	Self-assessment is accurate and explanation is detailed and clear.	Self-assessment is fairly accurate and explanation is clear.	Self-assessment is inaccurate and explanation is a little difficult to understand, but includes critical components.	Self-assessment is totally inaccurate and explanation is difficult to understand and is missing several components OR is not included.

Chapter 1 Project
Exponent Construction

Step 1 Fold one sheet of 8.5-inch by 11-inch paper in half and press firmly on the crease.

Step 2 Repeat the step of folding the paper in half as many times as you can.

Step 3 Unfold the paper and count the number of rectangles formed by the fold lines.

Step 4 Record your results in the table on the Student Recording Sheet.

Step 5 Count how many rectangles it takes to fill up different portions of the page as indicated in the table on the Student Recording Sheet.

Step 6 Record the results in exponential notation in the table on the Student Recording Sheet.

Step 7 Answer the questions on the Student Recording Sheet.

Chapter 1 Project
Student Recording Sheet

Total Number of Rectangles

Portion of Page	Number of Rectangles in Exponential Notation
1	
$\dfrac{1}{2}$	
$\dfrac{1}{4}$	

1. Which property(s) are you applying when completing the table?

2. Was it difficult to write the expressions in exponential notation?
   Which expressions, if any, were most difficult to write in exponential form?

3. What conclusion can you draw from your results?

2 Scientific Notation

Lesson 2.2 Activity: Addition and Subtraction with Scientific Notation

Teacher's Guide

Type of activity	Hands-on activity/game
Objective	Reinforce adding and subtracting numbers written in scientific notation.
Materials	• Scissors • 24 Expression cards on pages 15 and 16
Time	20–30 min
Ability levels	Mixed
Prerequisite skills	Use properties of exponents.
Grouping	Students should work in pairs.
Assessment of students' learning	See Lesson 2.2 Activity: Rubric.

Lesson 2.2 Activity
Rubric

Category	4	3	2	1
Mathematical concepts	Explanation shows complete understanding of the mathematical concepts used to solve the problem(s).	Explanation shows substantial understanding of the mathematical concepts used to solve the problem(s).	Explanation shows some understanding of the mathematical concepts needed to solve the problem(s).	Explanation shows very limited understanding of the underlying concepts needed to solve the problem(s) OR is not written.
Self-assessment	Self-assessment is accurate and explanation is detailed and clear.	Self-assessment is fairly accurate and explanation is clear.	Self-assessment is inaccurate and explanation is a little difficult to understand, but includes critical components.	Self-assessment is totally inaccurate and explanation is difficult to understand and is missing several components OR is not included.
Reflection	The reflection shows clear thought and effort. The learning experience being reflected upon is relevant to the student and learning goals.	The reflection shows a lot of thought and effort. Student makes attempts to demonstrate relevance, but the relevance is unclear in reference to learning goals.	The reflection shows some thought and effort. Some sections of the reflection are irrelevant to the student and/or learning goals.	The reflection is superficial. Most of the reflection is irrelevant to student and/or learning goals.

Lesson 2.2 Activity
Addition and Subtraction with Scientific Notation

Step 1   Cut out the cards provided by your teacher.

Step 2   Shuffle the cards and place them face down on the desk.

Step 3   The first player draws a card. First, decide if the expression must be rewritten so that the powers of 10 are the same. If it does, rewrite it in the appropriate space in the table. Next, use a property of exponents to combine the terms. Last, write the result in scientific notation. Write all the steps on the Student Recording Sheet. An example is shown below.

Expression	Rewrite the Expression	Use Properties of Exponents	Answer (in scientific notation)
$6.6 \cdot 10^6 - 3.5 \cdot 10^5$	$66 \cdot 10^5 - 3.5 \cdot 10^5$	$(66 - 3.5) \cdot 10^5$	$6.25 \cdot 10^6$

Step 4   The next player draws a card and repeats Step 3. Repeat the process until the table is filled.

Step 5   Your teacher will go through the correct answers with the class. Each correct answer in the table earns one point. There are no points for a wrong answer.

Step 6   Add up your points. The player with the most points is the winner.

Lesson 2.2 Activity
Student Recording Sheet

Expression	Rewrite the Expression	Use Properties of Exponents	Answer (in scientific notation)	Points
			Total points	

Self-Assessment and Reflection

1. Which expressions were the most difficult for you to simplify? What did you find the most difficult about these expressions?

2. What did you learn from this activity?

Lesson 2.2 Activity
Materials

$6.3 \cdot 10^{-5} - 3.3 \cdot 10^{-5}$	$2.3 \cdot 10^{3} + 1.8 \cdot 10^{3}$	$9.3 \cdot 10^{4} - 4.1 \cdot 10^{4}$
$2.2 \cdot 10^{-2} - 1.3 \cdot 10^{-3}$	$3.3 \cdot 10^{5} + 2.6 \cdot 10^{4}$	$8.7 \cdot 10^{5} - 2.1 \cdot 10^{4}$
$1.3 \cdot 10^{-3} - 3.4 \cdot 10^{-4}$	$4.5 \cdot 10^{7} + 7.6 \cdot 10^{6}$	$2.8 \cdot 10^{4} - 3.6 \cdot 10^{3}$
$5.5 \cdot 10^{-5} - 5.5 \cdot 10^{-6}$	$7.3 \cdot 10^{4} + 7.3 \cdot 10^{3}$	$6.6 \cdot 10^{6} - 6.6 \cdot 10^{5}$

Lesson 2.2 Activity continued
Materials

$4 \cdot 10^{-4} - 3.9 \cdot 10^{-5}$	$6 \cdot 10^6 + 0.5 \cdot 10^5$	$5 \cdot 10^5 - 4.5 \cdot 10^4$
$74 \cdot 10^{-5} - 2.4 \cdot 10^{-4}$	$89 \cdot 10^5 + 3.3 \cdot 10^6$	$53 \cdot 10^5 - 3.3 \cdot 10^6$
$5.4 \cdot 10^{-6} + 6.4 \cdot 10^{-6}$	$6.5 \cdot 10^{-4} + 4.2 \cdot 10^{-5}$	$3.2 \cdot 10^{-3} + 6.1 \cdot 10^{-4}$
$1 \cdot 10^{-4} + 0.3 \cdot 10^{-5}$	$48 \cdot 10^{-5} + 3.9 \cdot 10^{-4}$	$2.6 \cdot 10^{-5} + 2.6 \cdot 10^{-6}$

CHAPTER 2   Scientific Notation

Project: Scientific Notation Operations

Teacher's Guide

Common Core **Common Core State Standard**	8.EE4 Perform operations with numbers expressed in scientific notation, including problems where both decimal and scientific notation are used. Use scientific notation and choose units of appropriate size for measurements of very large or very small quantities.
Objective	Reinforce understanding of operations with scientific notation.
Material	Calculator
Time	20–30 min
Ability levels	Mixed
Prerequisite skills	Write numbers in scientific notation. Use properties of exponents.
Grouping	Students should work in small groups.
Assessment of students' learning	See Chapter 2 Project: Rubric.

Chapter 2 Project
Rubric

Category	4	3	2	1
Mathematical concepts	Explanation shows complete understanding of the mathematical concepts used to solve the problem(s).	Explanation shows substantial understanding of the mathematical concepts used to solve the problem(s).	Explanation shows some understanding of the mathematical concepts needed to solve the problem(s).	Explanation shows very limited understanding of the underlying concepts needed to solve the problem(s) OR is not written.
Mathematical reasoning	Uses complex and refined mathematical reasoning.	Uses effective mathematical reasoning.	Shows some evidence of mathematical reasoning.	Shows little evidence of mathematical reasoning.
Working with others	Student was an engaged partner, listening to suggestions of others and working cooperatively throughout the lesson.	Student was an engaged partner but had trouble listening to others and/or working cooperatively.	Student cooperated with others, but needed prompting to stay on task.	Student did not work effectively with others.

Chapter 2 Project
Scientific Notation Operations

Step 1   Refer to the table on the Student Recording Sheet. You are given 8 different expressions using the variables **A**, **B**, and **C**, in meters. Replace **A** with any number between 0 and 10 with 1 decimal place, **B** with any positive power of 10 listed below, and **C** with any negative power of 10 listed below.

10^3, 10^4, 10^5, 10^6, 10^7, 10^8, 10^9, 10^{-2}, 10^{-3}, 10^{-4}, 10^{-5}, 10^{-6}

Step 2   Write each expression with the appropriate unit in prefix form. Use the prefixes in the table below.

Prefix	micro-	milli-	centi-	kilo-	mega-	giga-
Symbol	μ	m	c	k	M	G
10^n	10^{-6}	10^{-3}	10^{-2}	10^3	10^6	10^9

Step 3   Evaluate each expression and complete the table on the Student Recording Sheet. An example is shown in the table.

Expression	Numerical Expression	Rewrite Expression	Prefix Form	Answer
$A \cdot B + A \cdot B$	$2.3 \cdot 10^4 + 2.2 \cdot 10^4$	$23 \cdot 10^3 + 22 \cdot 10^3$	23 km + 22 km	45 km

Step 4   Choose three of the expressions you created from the table and create a word problem for each one. Write them on the Student Recording Sheet.

Step 5   Trade word problems with another group and solve the ones they have written. Return your solutions to the other group for checking.

Name: _____ Date: _____

Chapter 2 Project
Student Recording Sheet

Expression	Numerical Expression	Rewrite Expression	Prefix Form	Answer
A · B + A · B				
A · B − A · B				
A · C + A · C				
A · C − A · C				
A · B · A · B				
A · C · A · C				
A · B ÷ A · B				
A · C ÷ A · C				

Word problem 1:

Word problem 2:

Word problem 3:

Answer the question.

1. Give some examples of prefixes used in measurements in everyday life. Why do we use prefixes to represent very large or very small numbers?

3 Algebraic Linear Equations

Lesson 3.1 Activity: Repeating Decimals

Teacher's Guide

Type of activity	Hands-on activity
Objective	Explore the relationship between certain repeating decimals and their equivalent fractions.
Material	Calculator (optional)
Time	20–30 min
Ability levels	Mixed
Prerequisite skills	Solve linear equations. Use a linear equation to write a repeating decimal as a fraction.
Grouping	Students should work alone or in pairs.
Assessment of students' learning	See Lesson 3.1 Activity: Rubric.

Lesson 3.1 Activity
Rubric

Category	4	3	2	1
Mathematical concepts	Explanation shows complete understanding of the mathematical concepts used to solve the problem(s).	Explanation shows substantial understanding of the mathematical concepts used to solve the problem(s).	Explanation shows some understanding of the mathematical concepts needed to solve the problem(s).	Explanation shows very limited understanding of the underlying concepts needed to solve the problem(s) OR is not written.
Mathematical reasoning	Uses complex and refined mathematical reasoning.	Uses effective mathematical reasoning.	Shows some evidence of mathematical reasoning.	Shows little evidence of mathematical reasoning.
Explanation	Explanation is detailed and clear.	Explanation is clear.	Explanation is a little difficult to understand, but includes critical components.	Explanation is difficult to understand and is missing several components OR is not included.

Lesson 3.1 Activity
Repeating Decimals

In this activity, you will explore the relationship between certain repeating decimals and the equivalent fractions. Complete Task A before beginning Task B. You may use a calculator to check your answers.

Task A

Step 1 Write each repeating decimal as a fraction, using a linear equation.

$0.\overline{1}$ $0.\overline{2}$ $0.\overline{3}$ $0.\overline{4}$

Show your work on the Student Recording Sheet. As you work through each equation, think about the following questions:

- How many repeating digits are there in the repeating decimal?
- What is the repeating digit?
- What should the decimal be multiplied by to eliminate the infinite string of digits?

Step 2 Record your answers on the Student Recording Sheet. What do you notice?

Step 3 Then, without using linear equations or your calculator, write each of the following repeating decimals as a fraction. Record your answers in the table on the Student Recording Sheet.

$0.\overline{5}$ $0.\overline{6}$ $0.\overline{7}$ $0.\overline{8}$

Step 4 Answer the questions on the Student Recording Sheet. Compare your answers with your partner's. Did you have the same conclusion?

Lesson 3.1 Activity continued
Repeating Decimals

Task B

Step 1 Write each repeating decimal as a fraction, using a linear equation.

$0.\overline{09}$ $0.\overline{18}$ $0.\overline{27}$ $0.\overline{36}$

Show your work on the Student Recording Sheet. As you work through each equation, think about the following questions:

- How many repeating digits are there in the repeating decimal?
- What are the repeating digits?
- What should the decimal be multiplied by to eliminate the infinite string of digits?

Step 2 Record your answers on the Student Recording Sheet. What do you notice?

Step 3 Then, without using linear equations or your calculator, write each of the following repeating decimals as a fraction. Record your answers in the table on the Student Recording Sheet.

$0.\overline{45}$ $0.\overline{54}$ $0.\overline{63}$ $0.\overline{72}$ $0.\overline{81}$ $0.\overline{90}$

Step 4 Answer the questions on the Student Recording Sheet. Compare your answers with your partner's. Did you have the same conclusion?

Lesson 3.1 Activity
Student Recording Sheet

Task A

Use a linear equation to write each repeating decimal as a fraction. Show all your work.

1. $0.\overline{1}$

2. $0.\overline{2}$

3. $0.\overline{3}$

4. $0.\overline{4}$

Complete the table without using a calculator or linear equations.

Repeating Decimal	$0.\overline{5}$	$0.\overline{6}$	$0.\overline{7}$	$0.\overline{8}$
Fraction				

5. What do you notice about the repeating decimals above?

6. Compare your answers with your partner. What can you conclude based on your observation?

Lesson 3.1 Activity continued
Student Recording Sheet

Task B

Use a linear equation to write each repeating decimal as a fraction. Show all your work.

7. $0.\overline{09}$

8. $0.\overline{18}$

9. $0.\overline{27}$

10. $0.\overline{36}$

Complete the table without using a calculator or linear equations.

Repeating Decimal	$0.\overline{45}$	$0.\overline{54}$	$0.\overline{63}$	$0.\overline{72}$	$0.\overline{81}$	$0.\overline{90}$
Fraction						

11. What do you notice about the repeating decimals above?

12. Compare your results with your partner. What can you conclude based on your observation?

CHAPTER 3 Algebraic Linear Equations

Project: Solving a Problem

Teacher's Guide

Common Core State Standard	8.EE8c Solve real-world and mathematical problems leading to two linear equations in two variables.
Objective	Reinforce the skill of constructing linear equations.
Material	Calculator
Time	20–30 min
Ability levels	Mixed
Prerequisite skills	Solve linear equations.
Grouping	Students should work in small groups.
Assessment of students' learning	See Chapter 3 Project: Rubric.

Chapter 3 Project
Rubric

Category	4	3	2	1
Mathematical concepts	Explanation shows complete understanding of the mathematical concepts used to solve the problem(s).	Explanation shows substantial understanding of the mathematical concepts used to solve the problem(s).	Explanation shows some understanding of the mathematical concepts needed to solve the problem(s).	Explanation shows very limited understanding of the underlying concepts needed to solve the problem(s) OR is not written.
Mathematical reasoning	Uses complex and refined mathematical reasoning.	Uses effective mathematical reasoning.	Shows some evidence of mathematical reasoning.	Shows little evidence of mathematical reasoning.
Strategy/ Procedures	Uses and efficient and effective strategy to solve the problem(s).	Uses an effective strategy to solve the problem(s).	Uses an effective strategy to solve the problem(s) but does not do it consistently.	Does not use an effective strategy to solve the problem(s).
Working with others	Student was an engaged partner, listening to suggestions of others and working cooperatively throughout the lesson.	Student was an engaged partner but had trouble listening to others and/or working cooperatively.	Student cooperated with others, but needed prompting to stay on task.	Student did not work effectively with others.

Chapter 3 Project
Solving a Problem

Claudia wants to rent a car for a trip. She calls two car rental companies to find out their rental rates for a particular vehicle. Mr. Wheel's Rentals charges a flat rate of $90 plus $0.10 per mile traveled. Grand Auto Rentals charges a flat rate of $75 plus $0.15 per mile traveled.

For this project, you will use linear equations with one variable to help Claudia to find the optimal solution in various situations.

Answer the question on the Student Recording Sheet

Chapter 3 Project
Student Recording Sheet

Show your work.

1. If Claudia plans to drive only 100 miles, which company should she choose?

2. For what driving distance would Claudia pay the same amount for both companies?

3. If Claudia has a budget of $130, which company should she choose in order to travel the further distance?

Lines and Linear Equations

Lesson 4.3 Activity: Writing Linear Equations

Teacher's Guide

Type of activity	Game
Objective	Practice writing linear equations.
Materials	• Scissors • One set of the expression cards on pages 35 and 36 for each pair of students
Time	20–30 min
Ability levels	Mixed
Prerequisite skills	Use the slope-intercept form of an equation for a line.
Grouping	Students should work in pairs.
Assessment of students' learning	See Lesson 4.3 Activity: Rubric.

Lesson 4.3 Activity
Rubric

Category	4	3	2	1
Mathematical concepts	Explanation shows complete understanding of the mathematical concepts used to solve the problem(s).	Explanation shows substantial understanding of the mathematical concepts used to solve the problem(s).	Explanation shows some understanding of the mathematical concepts needed to solve the problem(s).	Explanation shows very limited understanding of the underlying concepts needed to solve the problem(s) OR is not written.
Self-assessment	Self-assessment is accurate and explanation is detailed and clear.	Self-assessment is fairly accurate and explanation is clear.	Self-assessment is inaccurate and explanation is a little difficult to understand, but includes critical components.	Self-assessment is totally inaccurate and explanation is difficult to understand and is missing several components OR is not included.
Reflection	The reflection shows clear thought and effort. The learning experience being reflected upon is relevant to the student and learning goals.	The reflection shows a lot of thought and effort. Student makes attempts to demonstrate relevance, but the relevance is unclear in reference to learning goals.	The reflection shows some thought and effort. Some sections of the reflection are irrelevant to the student and/or learning goals.	The reflection is superficial. Most of the reflection is irrelevant to student and/or learning goals.

Lesson 4.3 Activity
Writing Linear Equations

Step 1   Cut out the cards provided by your teacher. Each card contains clues about a line.

Step 2   Shuffle the cards and place them face down on a desk or table.

Step 3   The first player draws a card. Use the clues on the card to write an equation in slope-intercept form for the line. Record the result in the table on the Student Recording Sheet.

Step 4   The second player draws a card and repeats Step 3.

Step 5   Continue the game until all the cards have been used.

Step 6   The player who writes the greatest number of correct linear equations is the winner.

Lesson 4.3 Activity
Student Recording Sheet

y = mx + b	Slope, m	y-intercept, b

Total score: _____

Self-Assessment and Reflection

1. Which type of information did you find easiest to use to write an equation? Explain what made it easiest for you.

2. Which type of information was most difficult for you to use to write an equation? Explain why you thought it was difficult.

3. What did you learn from this activity?

$6x + 2y = 7$	**Contains points (1, 2) and (2, 2)**	$m = 2; b = 5$	$m = -1;$ **Contains the point (0, 2)**
$3x - y = 8$	**Contains points (−2, 1) and (2, −3)**	$m = \frac{1}{3}; b = \frac{1}{2}$	$m = 3;$ **Contains the point (6, 2)**
$8y + 3x = 5$	**Contains points (0, 5) and (7, 0)**	$m = -4; b = -2$	$m = -3;$ **Contains the point (9, 0)**

$5y - 2x = 6$	**Contains points (9, 0) and (0, 4)**	$m = -\frac{1}{4}; b = -\frac{1}{2}$	$m = \frac{1}{2};$ **Contains the point (2, 6)**
$4y = 9 + x$	**Contains points (−3, 4) and (5, 2)**	$m = -3; b = \frac{2}{5}$	$m = -\frac{1}{4};$ **Contains the point (4, 8)**

Lesson 4.4 Activity: Sketching Graphs of Linear Equations

Teacher's Guide

Type of activity	Graphing calculator activity
Objective	Reinforce the concept of how the slope of a line describes its steepness.
Materials	• Graphing calculator • Pencil • Ruler
Time	20–30 min
Ability levels	Mixed
Prerequisite skills	Find the slope of a line, given the equation.
Grouping	Students should work in pairs or in small groups.
Assessment of students' learning	See Lesson 4.4 Activity: Rubric.

Lesson 4.4 Activity
Rubric

Category	4	3	2	1
Mathematical concepts	Explanation shows complete understanding of the mathematical concepts used to solve the problem(s).	Explanation shows substantial understanding of the mathematical concepts used to solve the problem(s).	Explanation shows some understanding of the mathematical concepts needed to solve the problem(s).	Explanation shows very limited understanding of the underlying concepts needed to solve the problem(s) OR is not written.
Mathematical reasoning	Uses complex and refined mathematical reasoning.	Uses effective mathematical reasoning.	Shows some evidence of mathematical reasoning.	Shows little evidence of mathematical reasoning.
Working with others	Student was an engaged partner, listening to suggestions of others and working cooperatively throughout the lesson.	Student was an engaged partner but had trouble listening to others and/or working cooperatively.	Student cooperated with others, but needed prompting to stay on task.	Student did not work effectively with others.
Reflection	The reflection shows clear thought and effort. The learning experience being reflected upon is relevant and meaningful to student and learning goals.	The reflection shows a lot of thought and effort. Student makes attempts to demonstrate relevance, but the relevance is unclear in reference to learning goals.	The reflection shows some thought and effort. Some sections of the reflection are irrelevant to the student and/or learning goals.	The reflection is superficial. Most of the reflection is irrelevant to student and/or learning goals.

Lesson 4.4 Activity
Sketching Graphs of Linear Equations

Use graph paper or a graphing calculator to graph each equation on the Student Recording Sheet.

Note: Some of the equations must be graphed on paper.

To use a graphing calculator, follow Steps 1 to 3:

Step 1   Press [Y=] to display the Y= Editor.

Step 2   Enter the equation in the table on the Student Recording Sheet.

Step 3   Press [GRAPH] to graph the equation.

Step 4   Sketch the graph in the table on the Student Recording Sheet.

Step 5   Answer the questions on the Student Recording Sheet.

Lesson 4.4 Activity
Student Recording Sheet

Equation	Graph
$y = \dfrac{3}{4}x + 1$	
$y = 5x - 2$	
$y = -\dfrac{1}{2}x - \dfrac{2}{3}$	
$y = 7 - 4x$	

Lesson 4.4 Activity continued
Student Recording Sheet

Equation	Graph
$y = \dfrac{2}{3}$	
$x = 8$	
$y = -2$	
$x = -\dfrac{5}{6}$	

Lesson 4.4 Activity continued
Student Recording Sheet

1. Which lines have positive slopes? What do their graphs have in common?

2. Which lines have negative slopes? What do their graphs have in common?

3. Which lines have undefined slope? Are you able to graph these lines on the graphing calculator? What do their graphs have in common?

4. Which lines have a slope of 0? What do their graphs look like?

Reflection

5. What conclusion(s) can you draw from your graphs?

CHAPTER 4 Lines and Linear Equations

Project: Exercise Rates

Teacher's Guide

Common Core	
Common Core State Standard	8.EE6 Use similar triangles to explain why the slope m is the same between any two distinct points on a non-vertical line in the coordinate plane; derive the equation $y = mx$ for a line through the origin and the equation $y = mx + b$ for a line intercepting the vertical axis at b.
Objective	Practice creating a graph and write an equation for various linear equations.
Materials	• Graph paper • Ruler
Time	20–30 min
Ability levels	Mixed
Prerequisite skills	Sketching graphs of linear equations.
Grouping	Students should work in groups of five.
Assessment of students' learning	See Chapter 4 Project: Rubric.

Chapter 4 Project
Rubric

Category	4	3	2	1
Mathematical concepts	Explanation shows complete understanding of the mathematical concepts used to solve the problem(s).	Explanation shows substantial understanding of the mathematical concepts used to solve the problem(s).	Explanation shows some understanding of the mathematical concepts needed to solve the problem(s).	Explanation shows very limited understanding of the underlying concepts needed to solve the problem(s) OR is not written.
Mathematical reasoning	Uses complex and refined mathematical reasoning.	Uses effective mathematical reasoning.	Shows some evidence of mathematical reasoning.	Shows little evidence of mathematical reasoning.
Working with others	Student was an engaged partner, listening to suggestions of others and working cooperatively throughout the lesson.	Student was an engaged partner but had trouble listening to others and/or working cooperatively.	Student cooperated with others, but needed prompting to stay on task.	Student did not work effectively with others.

Chapter 4 Project
Exercise Rates

Step 1   Choose a method of exercise (walking, jogging, running, or biking) from the table on the Student Recording Sheet, and either research the rate at which you could exercise by that method, or use the one given in the table. Complete the table of values, using the rate that you chose.

Step 2   Choose an appropriate scale and graph the points from your table of values on graph paper. Use a ruler to draw a line through the points, and extend it so it passes through the origin.

Step 3   Answer the questions on the Student Recording Sheet.

Chapter 4 Project
Student Recording Sheet

Method	Rate (mi/h)
Walking	3
Jogging	5
Running	6
Biking	8

Time (x minutes)	15	30	45	60	120
Distance (y miles)					

1. For each data point, draw a vertical line from the point to the x-axis. The sides of each right triangle drawn are x and y. For each data point, find the ratio $\frac{y}{x}$. What do you notice about these ratios?

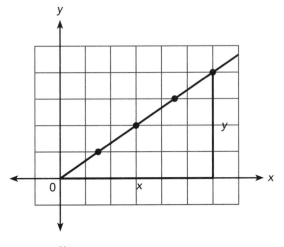

2. Choose two of the data points and draw another right triangle, using the points as the vertices at the acute angles, as shown in the diagram. Find the lengths of the horizontal and vertical sides of the triangle, then find the ratio $\frac{\text{Length of vertical side}}{\text{Length of horizontal side}}$. What do you notice about this ratio?

Choose another two different data points and use them to find another right triangle. Find the ratio $\frac{\text{Length of vertical side}}{\text{Length of horizontal side}}$ for this triangle. Is the result the same as the previous one?

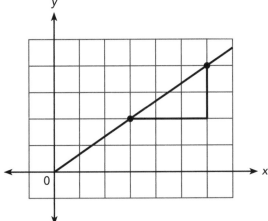

3. What is the slope of the line? What does it mean in terms of the triangles drawn, and in terms of the rate of exercise?

4. Suppose you add 1 mile to each of the y-coordinates in your table of values. How would the graph change? Would the slope change? Explain why or why not?

5 Systems of Linear Equations

Lesson 5.2 Activity: Equation Concentration

Teacher's Guide

Type of activity	Hands-on activity/game
Objective	Reinforce elimination method and substitution method.
Materials	• Scissors • One set of algebraic expression cards on pages 51 and 52
Time	20–30 min
Ability levels	Mixed
Prerequisite skills	Solve linear equations.
Grouping	Students should work in pairs.
Assessment of students' learning	See Lesson 5.2 Activity: Rubric.

Lesson 5.2 Activity
Rubric

Category	4	3	2	1
Mathematical concepts	Explanation shows complete understanding of the mathematical concepts used to solve the problem(s).	Explanation shows substantial understanding of the mathematical concepts used to solve the problem(s).	Explanation shows some understanding of the mathematical concepts needed to solve the problem(s).	Explanation shows very limited understanding of the underlying concepts needed to solve the problem(s) OR is not written.
Mathematical reasoning	Uses complex and refined mathematical reasoning.	Uses effective mathematical reasoning.	Shows some evidence of mathematical reasoning.	Shows little evidence of mathematical reasoning.
Reflection	The reflection shows clear thought and effort. The learning experience being reflected upon is relevant and meaningful to student and learning goals.	The reflection shows a lot of thought and effort. Student makes attempts to demonstrate relevance, but the relevance is unclear in reference to learning goals.	The reflection shows some thought and effort. Some sections of the reflection are irrelevant to student and/or learning goals.	The reflection is superficial. Most of the reflection is irrelevant to student and/or learning goals.

Name: _____   Date: _____

Lesson 5.2 Activity
Equation Concentration

Step 1 Cut out the cards provided by your teacher.

Step 2 Shuffle the equation cards and place them face down in 4 rows of 3 cards each.

Step 3 One player turns over two cards. If they show different versions of the same equation, keep the cards and write the equations in the table on the Student Recording Sheet. If they don't, turn the cards face down, the other player takes a turn.

Example:

System of Equations	Player 1 (Elimination Method)	Player 2 (Substitution Method)
	Equation 1 in ready-to-combine Form	Equation 1 in ready-to-substitute Form
$x + y = 10$ $x - 2y = 4$	$2x + 2y = 20$	$x = 10 - y$

Step 4 Continue playing until the table on the Student Recording Sheet is completed.

Step 5 The player who wrote the most number of equations is the winner.

Step 6 Answer the questions on the Student Recording Sheet.

Name: _____ Date: _____

Lesson 5.2 Activity
Student Recording Sheet

System of Equations	Player 1 (Elimination Method)	Player 2 (Substitution Method)
	Equation 1 in ready-to-combine Form	Equation 1 in ready-to-substitute Form
$x + y = 8$ $2x + y = 11$		
$3x + y = 9$ $2y - 3x = 5$		
$x + y = 7$ $x + 2y = 12$		
$x + y = 6$ $3x - y = 2$		
$2x + y = 7$ $2y - 2x = 2$		
$x + 2y = 9$ $2x + 2y = 10$		

1. Choose one of the systems in the table and solve it both by elimination and by substitution. Which method do you think is easier? Explain your choice.

2. Are there other equations which you can use to solve the questions for each of the methods? Give an example.

Reflection

3. What conclusion can you draw from the game?

Lesson 5.2 Activity
Materials

Elimination equation cards

$2x + 2y = 16$	$6x + 2y = 18$	$2x + 2y = 14$
$3x + 3y = 18$	$4x + 2y = 14$	$2x + 4y = 18$

Lesson 5.2 Activity continued
Materials

Substitution equation cards

$x = 8 - y$	$3x = 9 - y$	$x = 7 - y$
$y = 6 - x$	$2x = 7 - y$	$2y = 9 - x$

CHAPTER 5 Systems of Linear Equations

Project: Solving Linear Equations by Algebraic and Graphing Methods

Teacher's Guide

Common Core	
Common Core State Standard	8.EE8b Solve systems of two linear equations in two variables algebraically, and estimate solutions by graphing the equations.
Objective	Reinforce algebraic and graphical solving skills.
Material	Calculator
Time	20–30 min
Ability levels	Advanced
Prerequisite skills	Solve equations using both algebraic and graphing methods.
Grouping	Students should work in pairs or in small groups.
Assessment of students' learning	See Chapter 5 Project: Rubric.

© Marshall Cavendish International (Singapore) Private Limited.

Chapter 5 Project
Rubric

Category	4	3	2	1
Mathematical concepts	Explanation shows complete understanding of the mathematical concepts used to solve the problem(s).	Explanation shows substantial understanding of the mathematical concepts used to solve the problem(s).	Explanation shows some understanding of the mathematical concepts needed to solve the problem(s).	Explanation shows very limited understanding of the underlying concepts needed to solve the problem(s) OR is not written.
Mathematical reasoning	Uses complex and refined mathematical reasoning.	Uses effective mathematical reasoning.	Shows some evidence of mathematical reasoning.	Show little evidence of mathematical reasoning.
Explanation	Explanation is detailed and clear.	Explanation is clear.	Explanation is a little difficult to understand, but includes critical components.	Explanation is difficult to understand and is missing several components OR is not included.
Working with others	Student was an engaged partner, listening to suggestions of others and working cooperatively throughout the lesson.	Student was an engaged partner but had trouble listening to others and/or working cooperatively.	Student cooperated with others, but needed prompting to stay on task.	Student did not work effectively with others.

Chapter 5 Project
Solving Linear Equations by Algebraic and Graphing Methods

Step 1   Graph the equations $x + y = 6$ and $3x - y = 2$.

Step 2   Find the coordinates of the point where the two lines intersect.

Step 3   Draw another line that contains the point of intersection. Find an equation for this line.

Step 4   Draw a line on the graph that creates an inconsistent system of equations with any of the previous equations.

Step 5   Draw a line on the graph that creates a dependent system of equations with any of the previous equations.

Step 6   Answer the questions on the Student Recording Sheet.

Chapter 5 Project
Student Recording Sheet

1. Solve the original system of linear equations using either the substitution method or the elimination method. Does the solution correspond to the point of intersection on your graph?

2. Write an equation for the third line. Write a system of equations using this line and either of the two previous equations. Does this system have the same solution as the original system? Why or why not?

3. Write an equation for the line that creates an inconsistent system of equations. What is the slope of this line? Which of the first three lines has the same slope?

4. Write an equation for the line that creates a dependent system of equations. Which of the previous equations is it most like?

5. Compare your graph with the other groups' graphs. Do they have the same characteristics?

Functions

Lesson 6.2 Activity: Function Representation

Teacher's Guide

Type of activity	Hands-on activity
Objective	Represent a function in different forms.
Materials	• Thermometer with Celsius and Fahrenheit scales (optional) • Picture of a thermometer on page 61 • Grid paper on page 62
Time	20–30 min
Ability levels	Mixed
Prerequisite skills	Explain slope and *y*-intercept in the context of real-world problems; find the equation for a line.
Grouping	Student may work alone or in pairs.
Assessment of students' learning	See Lesson 6.2 Activity: Rubric.
Preparation	Make sufficient copies of the grid paper on page 62 before the activity.

Lesson 6.2 Activity
Rubric

Category	4	3	2	1
Mathematical concepts	Explanation shows complete understanding of the mathematical concepts used to solve the problem(s).	Explanation shows substantial understanding of the mathematical concepts used to solve the problem(s).	Explanation shows some understanding of the mathematical concepts needed to solve the problem(s).	Explanation shows very limited understanding of the underlying concepts needed to solve the problem(s) OR is not written.
Mathematical reasoning	Uses complex and refined mathematical reasoning.	Uses effective mathematical reasoning.	Shows some evidence of mathematical reasoning.	Shows little evidence of mathematical reasoning.
Explanation	Explanation is detailed and clear.	Explanation is clear.	Explanation is a little difficult to understand, but includes critical components.	Explanation is difficult to understand and is missing several components OR is not included.

Lesson 6.2 Activity
Function Representation

In this activity, you will examine the relationship between the Fahrenheit and Celsius temperature scales.

Step 1   Use the picture of a thermometer to complete the table of temperatures on the Student Recording Sheet as accurately as you can.

Step 2   If you have a thermometer that measures temperature in both Fahrenheit and Celsius, use it to measure the temperatures of other substances. Record your results in the table on the Student Recording Sheet.

Step 3   Answer the questions on the Student Recording Sheet.

Lesson 6.2 Activity
Student Recording Sheet

Object	Temperature (°C)	Temperature (°F)
Boiling water	100	212
Ice cube	0	32
Normal human body temperature		98.6
Room temperature		70
Chilled orange juice	13.9	

1. What do you notice about the Fahrenheit and Celsius scales on the thermometer?

2. Use your table of values to graph the points on the grid paper on page 60. Use 1 unit on the horizontal axis to represent 10°C, and 1 unit on the vertical axis to represent 50°F. Connect the points to make a straight line.

3. Write an algebraic equation for the linear function whose input is a temperature in °C and whose output is the corresponding temperature in °F.

Reflection

4. Explain what the slope and y-intercept of your graph represent in terms of the two different temperature scales.

Lesson 6.2 Activity
Materials

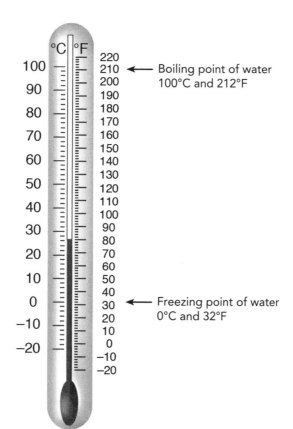

Boiling point of water
100°C and 212°F

Freezing point of water
0°C and 32°F

Lesson 6.2 Activity continued
Materials

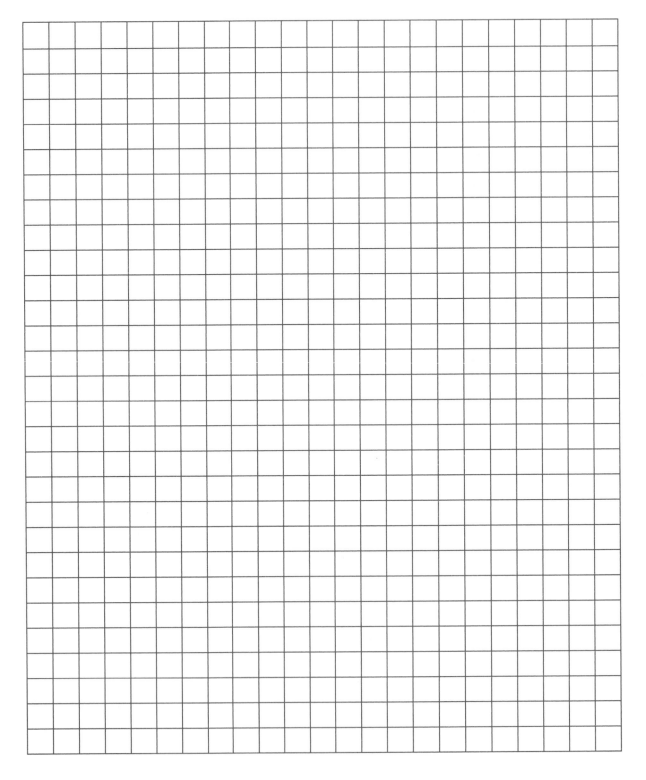

CHAPTER 6 Functions

Project: Nonlinear Functions

Teacher's Guide

Common Core	
Common Core State Standard	8.F5 Describe qualitatively the functional relationship between two quantities by analyzing a graph.
Objective	Identify nonlinear functions from graphs.
Materials	• Pencil • Paper
Time	20–30 min
Ability levels	Mixed
Prerequisite skills	Represent a function as a graph.
Grouping	Student should work in pairs or in small groups.
Assessment of students' learning	See Chapter 6 Project: Rubric.

Chapter 6 Project
Rubric

Category	4	3	2	1
Mathematical concepts	Explanation shows complete understanding of the mathematical concepts used to solve the problem(s).	Explanation shows substantial understanding of the mathematical concepts used to solve the problem(s).	Explanation shows some understanding of the mathematical concepts needed to solve the problem(s).	Explanation shows very limited understanding of the underlying concepts needed to solve the problem(s) OR is not written.
Mathematical reasoning	Uses complex and refined mathematical reasoning.	Uses effective mathematical reasoning.	Shows some evidence of mathematical reasoning.	Shows little evidence of mathematical reasoning.
Working with others	Student was an engaged partner, listening to suggestions of others and working cooperatively throughout the lesson.	Student was an engaged partner but had trouble listening to others and/or working cooperatively.	Student cooperated with others, but needed prompting to stay on task.	Student did not work effectively with others.
Explanation	Explanation is detailed and clear.	Explanation is clear.	Explanation is a little difficult to understand, but includes critical components.	Explanation is difficult to understand and is missing several components OR is not included.
Reflection	The reflection shows clear thought and effort. The learning experience being reflected upon is relevant and meaningful to student and learning goals.	The reflection shows a lot of thought and effort. Student makes attempts to demonstrate relevance, but the relevance is unclear in reference to learning goals.	The reflection shows some thought and effort. Some sections of the reflection are irrelevant to student and/or learning goals.	The reflection is superficial. Most of the reflection is irrelevant to student and/or learning goals.

Chapter 6 Project
Nonlinear Functions

Each graph below represents the distance between a person and his home. The person can travel at a constant rate to or away from his home. Complete Steps 1 and 2 for each graph. An example is shown on the Student Recording Sheet.

Step 1   List the type of slope (positive, negative, or zero) of each graph or section of the graph.

Step 2   Give a short description of the situation that the graph could represent in terms of the person traveling to and away from his home.

Step 3   Answer the questions on the Student Recording Sheet.

A.
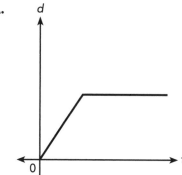

B.
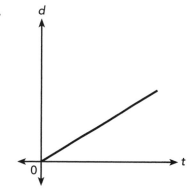

C.
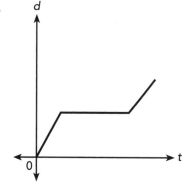

D.
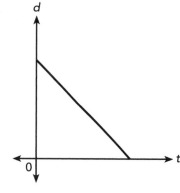

E.
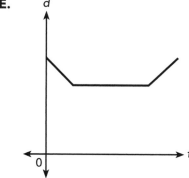

F.
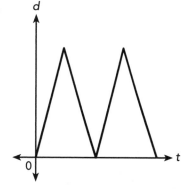

Chapter 6 Project
Student Recording Sheet

Graph	Type of Slope(s)	Description
A	Positive, zero	The person travels away from home, then stays in one place.
B		
C		
D		
E		
F		

1. Which of the graphs have a constant rate of change? What does this mean in terms of the situation?

2. What does a positive slope represent in terms of the situation?

3. What does a negative slope represent in terms of the situation?

4. What does a slope of zero represent in terms of the situation?

Reflection

5. Sketch a graph that represents this situation: A man wakes up at home, travels away from it, then returns home. Explain how you drew the graph.

The Pythagorean Theorem

Lesson 7.1 Activity: Use the Pythagorean Theorem and its Converse

Teacher's Guide

Type of activity	Hands-on activity
Objective	Reinforce the skill of applying the Pythagorean Theorem and its converse.
Materials	• Scissors • Glue • Ruler • A blank piece of colored paper
Time	20–30 min
Ability levels	Mixed
Prerequisite skills	Find the square of an integer. Use the Pythagorean Theorem.
Grouping	Students should work in pairs.
Assessment of students' learning	See Lesson 7.1 Activity: Rubric.

Lesson 7.1 Activity
Rubric

Category	4	3	2	1
Mathematical concepts	Explanation shows complete understanding of the mathematical concepts used to solve the problem(s).	Explanation shows substantial understanding of the mathematical concepts used to solve the problem(s).	Explanation shows some understanding of the mathematical concepts needed to solve the problem(s).	Explanation shows very limited understanding of the underlying concepts needed to solve the problem(s) OR is not written.
Reflection	The refection shows clear thought and effort. The learning experience being reflected upon is relevant and meaningful to student and learning goals.	The reflection shows a lot of thought and effort. Student makes attempts to demonstrate relevance, but the relevance is unclear in reference to learning goals.	The reflection shows some thought and effort. Some sections of the reflection are irrelevant to student and/or learning goals.	The reflection is superficial. Most of the reflection is irrelevant to student and/or learning goals.

Lesson 7.1 Activity
Use the Pythagorean Theorem and its Converse

Step 1   Measure, in centimeters, the length of each leg in each right triangle below.

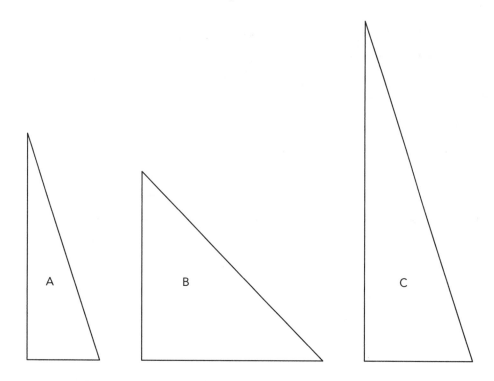

Step 2   Record the measurements in the table on the Student Recording Sheet.

Step 3   Copy and cut out the three right triangles.

Step 4   On a piece of colored paper, rearrange and paste the three right triangles so they enclose a colored right triangle. Your rearrangement must meet these conditions:

- The three triangles should not overlap.
- Exactly two vertices of each triangle should meet one vertex of another triangle.

Step 5   Answer the questions on the Student Recording Sheet.

Lesson 7.1 Activity
Student Recording Sheet

1. Use the Pythagorean Theorem to calculate the exact length of the hypotenuse of each right triangle. Show your work and record your answers in the table.

Right Triangle	Length of Vertical Leg (cm)	Length of Horizontal Leg (cm)	Length of Hypotenuse (cm)
A			
B			
C			

2. Explain why the enclosed triangle formed on the sheet of colored paper is a right triangle.

Reflection

3. Explain how you could cut out a right triangle from a piece of paper with hypotenuse exactly $\sqrt{80}$ centimeters long.

CHAPTER 7   The Pythagorean Theorem

Project: Apply the Distance Formula

Teacher's Guide

Common Core State Standard	8.G.8 Apply the Pythagorean Theorem to find the distance between two points in a coordinate system.
Objective	Reinforce the skill of applying the distance formula.
Material	Calculator
Time	20–30 min
Ability levels	Mixed
Prerequisite skills	Use the distance formula.
Grouping	Students should work in small groups.
Assessment of students' learning	See Chapter 7 Project: Rubric.

Chapter 7 Project
Rubric

Category	4	3	2	1
Mathematical concepts	Explanation shows complete understanding of the mathematical concepts used to solve the problem(s).	Explanation shows substantial understanding of the mathematical concepts used to solve the problem(s).	Explanation shows some understanding of the mathematical concepts needed to solve the problem(s).	Explanation shows very limited understanding of the underlying concepts needed to solve the problem(s) OR is not written.
Mathematical reasoning	Uses complex and refined mathematical reasoning.	Uses effective mathematical reasoning.	Shows some evidence of mathematical reasoning.	Shows little evidence of mathematical reasoning.
Neatness and organization	The work is presented in a neat, clear, organized fashion that is easy to read.	The work is presented in a neat and organized fashion that is usually easy to read.	The work is presented in an organized fashion but may be hard to read at times.	The work appears sloppy and unorganized. It is hard to know what information goes together.
Working with others	Student was an engaged partner, listening to suggestions of others and working cooperatively throughout the lesson.	Student was an engaged partner but had trouble listening to others and/or working cooperatively.	Student cooperated with others, but needed prompting to stay on task.	Student did not work effectively with others.

Chapter 7 Project
Apply the Distance Formula

Mrs. Smith lives in a small town. One morning, she plans to run the following errands. They are not listed in order.

- Take some clothing to the dry cleaner.
- Buy medicine at the pharmacy.
- Buy vegetables and fruits from either the grocery store or the supermarket.
- Have breakfast at either Kay's Café or Gourmet Inn.

On the diagram below, the positions of Mrs. Smith's house and the shops are shown as points on a coordinate place, where each unit represents 100 meters. The diagram is not drawn to scale. Mrs. Smith can walk directly from one location to another. All the shops have the same opening hours. She will return home after completing all the errands.

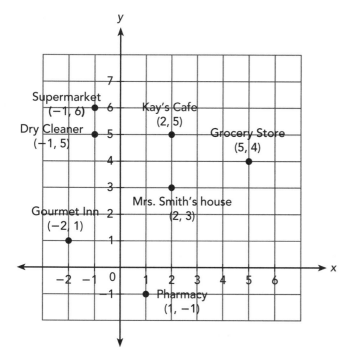

For this project, you will plan the order for her errands that you think is best. Present the route that you have chosen for Mrs. Smith to the class. Explain how you chose it.

Answer the questions on the Student Recording Sheet.

Chapter 7 Project
Student Recording Sheet

1. Write down the route for Mrs. Smith that you have planned.

2. Calculate the total distance that Mrs. Smith has to walk if she follows your route.

3. Describe any considerations in your planning.

8 Geometric Transformations

Lessons 8.1–8.3 Activity: Translations, Reflections, and Rotations

Teacher's Guide

Type of activity	Hands-on activity
Objective	Reinforce the understanding of translations, reflections, and rotations.
Materials	• Pictures I and II on pages 79 and 80 • Picture on page 81 • Picture on page 82 • Timer and buzzer, or a clock with a second hand
Time	20 min
Ability levels	Mixed
Prerequisite skills	Recognize geometric translations, reflections, and rotations.
Grouping	Students should work in pairs.
Assessment of students' learning	See Lessons 8.1–8.3 Activity: Rubric.

Lessons 8.1–8.3 Activity Rubric

Category	4	3	2	1
Mathematical concepts	Explanation shows complete understanding of the mathematical concepts used to solve the problem(s).	Explanation shows substantial understanding of the mathematical concepts used to solve the problem(s).	Explanation shows some understanding of the mathematical concepts needed to solve the problem(s).	Explanation shows very limited understanding of the underlying concepts needed to solve the problem(s) OR is not written.
Self-assessment	Self-assessment is accurate and explanation is detailed and clear.	Self-assessment is fairly accurate and explanation is clear.	Self-assessment is inaccurate and explanation is a little difficult to understand, but includes critical components.	Self-assessment is totally inaccurate and explanation is difficult to understand and is missing several components OR is not included.
Reflection	The reflection shows clear thought and effort. The learning experience being reflected upon is relevant and meaningful to student and learning goals.	The reflection shows a lot of thought and effort. Student makes attempts to demonstrate relevance, but the relevance is unclear in reference to learning goals.	The reflection shows some thought and effort. Some sections of the reflection are irrelevant to student and/or learning goals.	The reflection is superficial. Most of the reflection is irrelevant to student and/or learning goals.

Lessons 8.1–8.3 Activity
Translations, Reflection, and Rotations

This activity consists of three short tasks. The three tasks are timed. When each time is up, your teacher will let you know. Work on each task alone. You will discuss your answers with your partner after completing each task.

Task A

Use Picture I on page 79 and Picture II on page 80.
Pictures I and II are almost identical except for some differences. One geometric transformation (translation, reflection, or rotation) has been applied to some parts of Picture I. These objects have been replaced with their images in Picture II.

Identify all the transformed objects. Circle the object and its image, and number the object and its image on both Picture I and II. Complete the table under Task A on the Student Recording Sheet by listing the corresponding geometric transformation. You will have two minutes for this task.

Task B

Use the picture on page 81.
It shows the reflection of a word in the vertical line. Write the word on the Student Recording Sheet. You will have one minute for this task.

Task C

Use the picture on page 82.
It shows some letters of the alphabet and their images after a reflection in the vertical line. However, some of the images are wrong. Identify all the wrong images and give the correct corresponding image by completing the table under Task C on the Student Recording Sheet. You will have two minutes for this task.

Lessons 8.1–8.3 Activity
Student Recording Sheet

Task A

Object Number	Type of Geometric Transformation

Task B

Word: _____

Task C

Wrong Image	Correct Image

Self-Assessment and Reflection

1. Which skills were easiest for you, identifying geometric transformations, identifying images, or drawing images after geometric transformations? Explain.

2. In which skill(s) do you need more practice? Why do you think so?

3. What did you learn from this activity?

Picture I

Picture II

Text on truck:

MOVING HOUSE?

ENGAGE RD MOVERS AT

AN AFFORDABLE COST.

ENSURES HASSLE FREE

EXPERIENCE.

CALL 45908978456.

Lessons 8.1–8.3 Activity continued
Materials

REWARD

Wd	Wq
HT	HT
TZ	ZT
AM	MA
PM	MP

Lesson 8.3 Activity: Rotations

Teacher's Guide

Type of activity	Hands-on activity
Objective	Reinforce the understanding of half-turns.
Materials	• Paper • Pencil
Time	15 min
Ability levels	Mixed
Prerequisite skills	Understand the definition of a rotation.
Grouping	Students should work in pairs or small groups.
Assessment of students' learning	See Lesson 8.3 Activity: Rubric.

Lesson 8.3 Activity
Rubric

Category	4	3	2	1
Mathematical concepts	Explanation shows complete understanding of the mathematical concepts used to solve the problem(s).	Explanation shows substantial understanding of the mathematical concepts used to solve the problem(s).	Explanation shows some understanding of the mathematical concepts needed to solve the problem(s).	Explanation shows very limited understanding of the underlying concepts needed to solve the problem(s) OR is not written.
Reflection	The reflection shows clear thought and effort. The learning experience being reflected upon is relevant and meaningful to student and learning goals.	The reflection shows a lot of thought and effort. Student makes attempts to demonstrate relevance, but the relevance is unclear in reference to learning goals.	The reflection shows some thought and effort. Some sections of the reflection are irrelevant to student and/or learning goals.	The reflection is superficial. Most of the reflection is irrelevant to student and/or learning goals.

Lesson 8.3 Activity
Rotations

Step 1   Below are some letters and numbers. Turn this page upside down and look at the resulting images.

A   B   H   X   5   6   7   8   9

Step 2   Copy the resulting images on the Student Recording Sheet. The first one has been done for you.

Step 3   Study the following scenario.
A factory uses the following numbering system to label its products. The product code is printed on a sticker and pasted on the product before sending to the Quality department for inspection. The product code has this format:

_____ - _____ - _____

The first and last symbols are letters taken from the list {A, B, H, X} and the middle three symbols are three numbers taken from the list {5, 6, 7, 8, 9}. All letters and numbers in the product code are distinct. Also, the letters are in alphabetical order and the numbers are in order from least to greatest.
For example, B-579-X is a legitimate product code while B-597-X, B-557-X, X-579-B and B-597-B are not legitimate codes.

One day, Peter accidentally pastes the sticker on a product upside down. The resulting product code is still readable and of the format

_____ - _____ - _____ . However, the resulting product code is no longer legitimate.

Step 4   Work out the original product code and write it on the Student Recording Sheet.

Lesson 8.3 Activity
Student Recording Sheet

Letters/Numbers	Images
A	∀
B	
H	
X	
5	
6	
7	
8	
9	

Original product code: _____

Reflection

1. Explain why the upside-down product code is not legitimate even though it is still readable and of the correct format.

2. Explain how you arrived at your answer for the original product code.

3. What is the main geometric transformation that corresponds to turning the product code upside down?

CHAPTER 8 Geometric Transformations

Project: Describing Geometric Transformations

Teacher's Guide

Common Core	
Common Core State Standard	8.G.3 Describe the effect of dilations, translations, rotations, and reflections on two-dimensional figures using coordinates.
Objective	Reinforce the skill of applying and describing geometric transformations.
Materials	• Diagram on page 91 • Diagram on page 92
Time	20–30 min
Ability levels	Mixed
Prerequisite skills	Recognize dilations, translations, reflections, and rotations.
Grouping	Students should work in small groups.
Assessment of students' learning	See Chapter 8 Project: Rubric.
Preparation	This project can be conducted in a computer lab. The students can use any geometry drawing software available to help them deduce a correct sequence of geometric transformations.

Chapter 8 Project
Rubric

Category	4	3	2	1
Mathematical concepts	Explanation shows complete understanding of the mathematical concepts used to solve the problem(s).	Explanation shows substantial understanding of the mathematical concepts used to solve the problem(s).	Explanation shows some understanding of the mathematical concepts needed to solve the problem(s).	Explanation shows very limited understanding of the underlying concepts needed to solve the problem(s) OR is not written.
Mathematical reasoning	Uses complex and refined mathematical reasoning.	Uses effective mathematical reasoning.	Shows some evidence of mathematical reasoning.	Shows little evidence of mathematical reasoning.
Organization	The work is presented in a neat, clear, organized fashion that is easy to read.	The work is presented in a neat and organized fashion that is usually easy to read.	The work is presented in an organized fashion but may be hard to read at times.	The work appears sloppy and unorganized. It is hard to know what information goes together.
Working with others	Student was an engaged partner, listening to suggestions of others and working cooperatively throughout the lesson.	Student was an engaged partner but had trouble listening to others and/or working cooperatively.	Student cooperated with others, but needed prompting to stay on task.	Student did not work effectively with others.

Chapter 8 Project
Describing Geometric Transformations

The figure on page 91 is drawn on the coordinate plane. The figure is made up of a circle, four parallelograms, one rectangle and a square.

In this project, you will form the figure in the same position by applying transformations to the shapes on page 92.

On the Student Recording Sheet, describe in detail the geometric transformation(s) needed to transform shapes A to F into the required figure. You must use all the shapes. Each shape can undergo more than one geometric transformation. The geometric transformations you can use are translations, reflections, rotations, and dilations.

Share your solution with the class.

Chapter 8 Project
Student Recording Sheet

Describe the geometric transformation(s) for each shape.

Shape A

Shape B

Shape C

Shape D

Shape E

Shape F

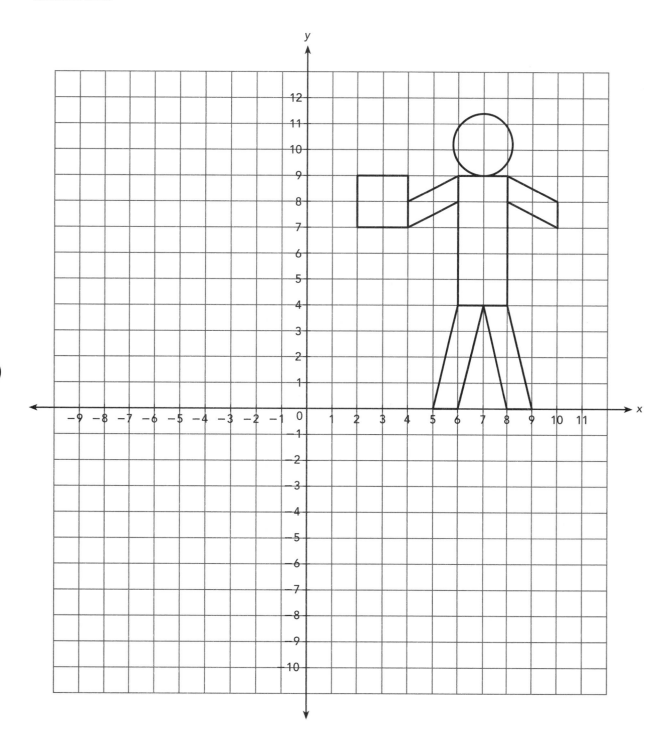

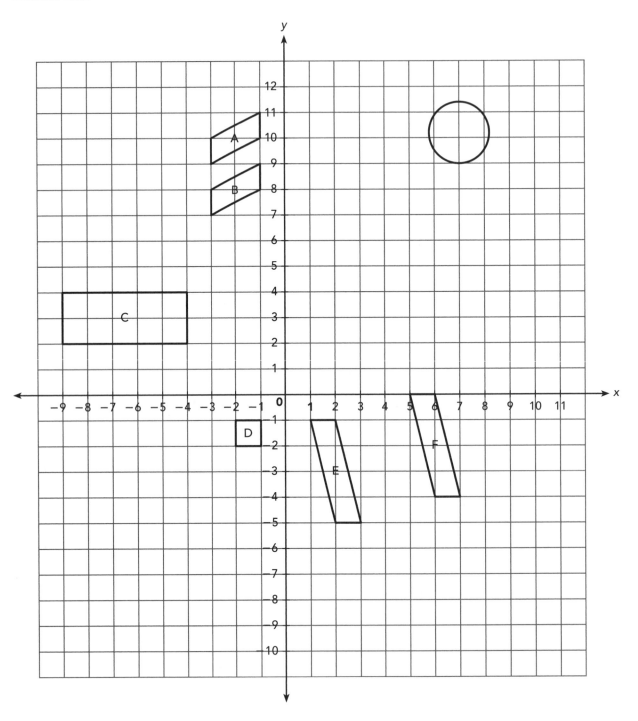

9 Congruence and Similarity

Lesson 9.2 Activity: Areas of Similar Figures

Teacher's Guide

Type of activity	Hands-on activity
Objective	Apply concept of similar triangles to make indirect measurements.
Material	Graph paper
Time	20–30 min
Ability levels	Mixed
Prerequisite skills	Know the definition of similar figures.
Grouping	Students should work in small groups.
Assessment of students' learning	See Lesson 9.2 Activity: Rubric.

Lesson 9.2 Activity
Rubric

Category	4	3	2	1
Mathematical concepts	Explanation shows complete understanding of the mathematical concepts used to solve the problem(s).	Explanation shows substantial understanding of the mathematical concepts used to solve the problem(s).	Explanation shows some understanding of the mathematical concepts needed to solve the problem(s).	Explanation shows very limited understanding of the underlying concepts needed to solve the problem(s) OR is not written.
Reflection	The reflection shows clear thought and effort. The learning experience being reflected upon is relevant and meaningful to student and learning goals.	The reflection shows a lot of thought and effort. Student makes attempts to demonstrate relevance, but the relevance is unclear in reference to learning goals.	The reflection shows some thought and effort. Some sections of the reflection are irrelevant to the student and/or learning goals.	The reflection is superficial. Most of the reflection is irrelevant to student and/or learning goals.

Lesson 9.2 Activity
Areas of Similar Figures

Step 1   Draw a small rectangle on graph paper and label it A. Find the lengths of its sides and its area and record them in the table on the Student Recording Sheet.

Step 2   Each student in the group should create another rectangle that is similar to rectangle A by choosing a scale factor and multiplying each side length of rectangle A by the scale factor. Label the new rectangles B, C, D, and so on. Find the area of each new rectangle. Record the side lengths and areas in the table on the Student Recording Sheet.

Example:

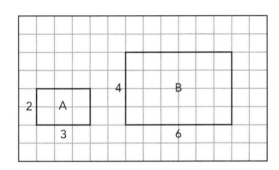

Rectangle	Scale Factor	Base	Height	Area
A	1	3	2	6
B	2	6	4	24

Step 3   Repeat Steps 1 and 2, starting with a right triangle instead of a rectangle.

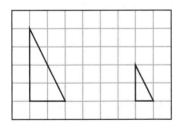

Step 4   Complete the tables and answer the questions on the Student Recording Sheet.

Lesson 9.2 Activity
Student Recording Sheet

Use your diagrams of similar figures to complete the tables.

Similar Rectangles

Rectangle	Scale Factor	Base	Height	Area
A	1			
B				
C				
D				

Similar Triangles

Triangle	Scale Factor	Base	Height	Area
A	1			
B				
C				
D				

1. Find the ratio of the area of rectangle B to the area of rectangle A.
   Compare this ratio to the scale factor for rectangle B and rectangle A.

2. Find the ratio of the area of each of the new rectangles to the area of
   rectangle A, and compare it to each of the scale factors. What do you
   notice?

3. Repeat Questions 1 and 2, using the similar right triangles.

Reflection

4. Suppose two similar polygons have a scale factor of s. What is the ratio of
   their areas? Explain your answer.

CHAPTER 9 Congruence and Similarity

Project: Relating Congruent Figures to Geometric Transformations

Teacher's Guide

Common Core (Common Core logo) **Common Core State Standard**	8.G.2 Understand that a two-dimensional figure is congruent to another if the second can be obtained from the first by a sequence of rotations, reflections, and translations: given two congruent figures, describe a sequence that exhibits the congruence between them.
	8.G.3 Describe the effect of dilations, translations, rotations, and reflections on two-dimensional figures using coordinates.
Objective	Reinforce the skill of applying and describing geometric transformations.
Material	Geometry software or graph paper
Time	20–30 min
Ability levels	Mixed
Prerequisite skills	• Understand the definitions of reflections and rotations. • Use basic functions of geometry software, such as creating a triangle, creating a line, and using transformation tools.
Grouping	Students should work in pairs.
Assessment of students' learning	See Chapter 9 Project: Rubric.
Preparation	This project can be completed with pencil and paper, or with geometry software.

Chapter 9 Project
Rubric

Category	4	3	2	1
Mathematical concepts	Explanation shows complete understanding of the mathematical concepts used to solve the problem(s).	Explanation shows substantial understanding of the mathematical concepts used to solve the problem(s).	Explanation shows some understanding of the mathematical concepts needed to solve the problem(s).	Explanation shows very limited understanding of the underlying concepts needed to solve the problem(s) OR is not written.
Mathematical reasoning	Uses complex and refined mathematical reasoning.	Uses effective mathematical reasoning.	Shows some evidence of mathematical reasoning.	Shows little evidence of mathematical reasoning.
Neatness and organization	The work is presented in a neat, clear, organized fashion that is easy to read.	The work is presented in a neat and organized fashion that is usually easy to read.	The work is presented in an organized fashion but may be hard to read at times.	The work appears sloppy and unorganized. It is hard to know what information goes together.
Working with others	Student was an engaged partner, listening to suggestions of others and working cooperatively throughout the lesson.	Student was an engaged partner but had trouble listening to others and/or working cooperatively.	Student cooperated with others, but needed prompting to stay on task.	Student did not work effectively with others.

Chapter 9 Project
Relating Congruent Figures to Geometric Transformations

Step 1   Open the geometry software on your computer, or use graph paper.

Step 2   Create or draw a triangle with vertices A (3, 6), B (3, 4), and C (6, 4).

Step 3   Draw a vertical line, $x = 1$.

Step 4   Reflect triangle ABC about the line $x = 1$ to obtain triangle $A'B'C'$.

Step 5   Draw a horizontal line, $y = 1$.

Step 6   Reflect triangle $A'B'C'$ about the line $y = 1$ to obtain triangle $A''B''C''$.

Step 7   Record the coordinates of points A'', B'', and C'' in the table on the Student Recording Sheet.

Step 8   Triangle ABC can also be mapped onto triangle $A''B''C''$ by a 180° rotation. Find the center of the rotation and write its coordinates in the table on the Student Recording Sheet.

Step 9   On a new set of axes, repeat Steps 3 through 8 for the different sets of vertical and horizontal lines listed in the table on the Student Recording Sheet.

Step 10   Answer the questions on the Student Recording Sheet.

Chapter 9 Project
Student Recording Sheet

Vertical Line	Horizontal Line	Coordinates of A"	Coordinates of B"	Coordinates of C"	Center of Rotation
$x = 1$	$y = 1$				
$x = 0$	$y = 0$				
$x = 2$	$y = 3$				
$x = -2$	$y = -1$				

1. Explain why triangle ABC is congruent to triangle $A"B"C"$ after each transformation.

2. What do you notice about the center of the rotation in each case?

3. Complete the following conclusion.

   Reflecting a figure in a vertical line $x = a$ and then in a horizontal line $y = b$ is equivalent to _____.

4. Does the order of the two reflections affect your conclusion in Question 3? Explain.

Statistics

Lessons 10.1–10.2 Activity: Modeling Linear Associations

Teacher's Guide

Type of activity	Computer activity
Objective	Reinforce the understanding of using an equation of a line of best fit to make estimates or predictions.
Materials	• Graphing calculator or spreadsheet software • A large piece of paper • Tape • Ruler/measuring tape
Time	20–30 min
Ability levels	Mixed
Prerequisite skills	• Construct a scatter plot from a data set. • Find an equation for a line of best fit for a data set, using a graphing calculator or spreadsheet software.
Grouping	Students should work in pairs (for data analysis) or in groups of six (for data collection).
Assessment of students' learning	See Lessons 10.1–10.2 Activity: Rubric.
Preparation	Make sure students have directions for making a scatter plot and finding a line of best fit on a graphing calculator or spreadsheet software. Divide the class into groups of six to facilitate data collection.

Lessons 10.1–10.2 Activity Rubric

Category	4	3	2	1
Mathematical concepts	Explanation shows complete understanding of the mathematical concepts used to solve the problem(s).	Explanation shows substantial understanding of the mathematical concepts used to solve the problem(s).	Explanation shows some understanding of the mathematical concepts needed to solve the problem(s).	Explanation shows very limited understanding of the underlying concepts needed to solve the problem(s) OR is not written.
Reflection	The reflection shows clear thought and effort. The learning experience being reflected upon is relevant and meaningful to student and learning goals.	The reflection shows a lot of thought and effort. Student makes attempts to demonstrate relevance, but the relevance is unclear in reference to learning goals.	The reflection shows some thought and effort. Some sections of the reflection are irrelevant to student and/or learning goals.	The reflection is superficial. Most of the reflection is irrelevant to student and/or learning goals.

Lessons 10.1–10.2 Activity
Modeling Linear Associations

Step 1   Tape the paper to the floor.

Step 2   Remove your shoes. Trace the outline of your foot on the paper.

Step 3   Draw straight lines touching the outermost points at the top, bottom, and both sides of the outline.

Step 4   Use the ruler or measuring tape to measure the length from the bottom line to the top line that you drew in Step 3.

Step 5   Repeat the drawing and measuring for everyone in your group. Record the foot lengths of each group member in the first table on the Student Recording Sheet.

Step 6   Measure the height of each group member and record it in the second table on the Student Recording Sheet.

Step 7   Enter the foot length and height data in a list or table on a graphing calculator or in spreadsheet software.

Step 8   Use the calculator or software to create a scatter plot of your data.

Step 9   Follow the instructions for the graphing calculator or software to graph the line of best fit for the data and find its equation.

Name: _____   Date: _____

Lessons 10.1–10.2 Activity
Student Recording Sheet

Name	Foot Length (x centimeters)	Height (y centimeters)

Equation of line of best fit: _____

Answer these questions. Show your work.

1. Look at your data. Are there any outliers? Describe the association between the heights and the foot lengths in the scatter plot.

2. Using the equation of the line of best fit to estimate values outside the range of the data is known as extrapolation. Give an example that shows that extrapolation may not lead to a valid estimate.

3. Use the equation of the line of best fit to estimate the height of a student whose foot length is 24 centimeters. Round your answer to the nearest centimeter. Do you think your estimate is a good one? Explain why or why not.

Reflection

4. What did you learn from this activity?

CHAPTER 10   Statistics

Project: Constructing and Interpreting Two-Way Tables

Teacher's Guide

Common Core ⊙ **Common Core State Standard**	8.SP.4 Understand that patterns of association can also be seen in bivariate categorical data by displaying frequencies in a two-way table. Construct and interpret a two-way table summarizing data on two categorical variables collected from the same objects. Use relative frequencies calculated for rows or columns to describe possible association between the two variables.
Objective	Reinforce the skill of summarizing and analyzing data by constructing a two-way table.
Materials	• One set of the information cards on pages 109 and 110 for each group • Two small boxes, envelopes, or bags for each group • Scissors
Time	20–30 min
Ability levels	Mixed
Prerequisite skills	• Construct a two-way table. • Convert data to relative frequencies in a two-way table.
Grouping	Students should work in small groups.
Assessment of students' learning	See Chapter 10 Project: Rubric.

Chapter 10 Project
Rubric

Category	4	3	2	1
Mathematical concepts	Explanation shows complete understanding of the mathematical concepts used to solve the problem(s).	Explanation shows substantial understanding of the mathematical concepts used to solve the problem(s).	Explanation shows some understanding of the mathematical concepts needed to solve the problem(s).	Explanation shows very limited understanding of the underlying concepts needed to solve the problem(s) OR is not written.
Mathematical reasoning	Uses complex and refined mathematical reasoning.	Uses effective mathematical reasoning.	Shows some evidence of mathematical reasoning.	Shows little evidence of mathematical reasoning.
Strategy/ Procedures	Uses an efficient and effective strategy to solve the problem(s).	Uses an effective strategy to solve the problem(s).	Uses an effective strategy to solve the problem(s) but does not do it consistently.	Does not use an effective strategy to solve the problem(s).
Working with others	Student was an engaged partner, listening to suggestions of others and working cooperatively throughout the lesson.	Student was an engaged partner but had trouble listening to others and/or working cooperatively.	Student cooperated with others, but needed prompting to stay on task.	Student did not work effectively with others.

Chapter 10 Project
Constructing and Interpreting Two-Way Tables

Mrs. Smith is trying to determine how many elective art classes to schedule at her school. She asks each student to complete a card and analyzes the data collected from a random sample of eleven males and nine females.

For this project, you will help Mrs. Smith to organize, summarize, and analyze the data collected from the random sample.

Step 1	Cut out the cards on pages 107 and 108.
Step 2	Sort the cards according to gender.
Step 3	Place the cards in two separate boxes, envelopes, or bags labeled "Female" and "Male".
Step 4	Mix the cards well in each box.
Step 5	Draw eleven cards from the box labeled "Male".
Step 6	Draw nine cards from the box labeled "Female".
Step 7	Answer the questions on the Student Recording Sheet.

Chapter 10 Project
Student Recording Sheet

1. How did Mrs. Smith randomly select the 20 students? What type of sampling method was used?

2. Summarize the data you collected in a two-way table.

3. Find the relative frequencies to compare the distribution of the genders for each class.

4. Describe the distribution of males and females for each class.

5. Another teacher working on scheduling suggests combining two two-way tables to form a single two-way table. Do you think this is a good suggestion? Why or why not?

Chapter 10 Project
Materials

Register Number: 1 **Name:** Alex **Gender:** Male **Preferred subject:** Digital Music	**Register Number:** 14 **Name:** Emma **Gender:** Female **Preferred subject:** Graphic Design	**Register Number:** 27 **Name:** Henry **Gender:** Male **Preferred subject:** Graphic Design	**Register Number:** 40 **Name:** Michael **Gender:** Male **Preferred subject:** Digital Music
Register Number: 2 **Name:** Beatrice **Gender:** Female **Preferred subject:** Graphic Design	**Register Number:** 15 **Name:** Frank **Gender:** Male **Preferred subject:** Drawing	**Register Number:** 28 **Name:** Howard **Gender:** Male **Preferred subject:** Vocal Music	**Register Number:** 41 **Name:** Martin **Gender:** Male **Preferred subject:** Vocal Music
Register Number: 3 **Name:** Alaina **Gender:** Female **Preferred subject:** Drawing	**Register Number:** 16 **Name:** Frederick **Gender:** Male **Preferred subject:** Digital Music	**Register Number:** 29 **Name:** Hubert **Gender:** Male **Preferred subject:** Digital Music	**Register Number:** 42 **Name:** Michelle **Gender:** Female **Preferred subject:** Drawing
Register Number: 4 **Name:** Adrian **Gender:** Male **Preferred subject:** Digital Music	**Register Number:** 17 **Name:** Gerard **Gender:** Male **Preferred subject:** Digital Music	**Register Number:** 30 **Name:** James **Gender:** Male **Preferred subject:** Drawing	**Register Number:** 43 **Name:** Phillip **Gender:** Male **Preferred subject:** Digital Music
Register Number: 5 **Name:** Billy **Gender:** Male **Preferred subject:** Digital Music	**Register Number:** 18 **Name:** George **Gender:** Male **Preferred subject:** Vocal Music	**Register Number:** 31 **Name:** Jeffrey **Gender:** Male **Preferred subject:** Drawing	**Register Number:** 44 **Name:** Ryan **Gender:** Male **Preferred subject:** Vocal Music
Register Number: 6 **Name:** Cassandra **Gender:** Female **Preferred subject:** Vocal Music	**Register Number:** 19 **Name:** Glenda **Gender:** Female **Preferred subject:** Digital Music	**Register Number:** 32 **Name:** Jane **Gender:** Female **Preferred subject:** Digital Music	**Register Number:** 45 **Name:** Sally **Gender:** Female **Preferred subject:** Vocal Music
Register Number: 7 **Name:** Chloe **Gender:** Female **Preferred subject:** Graphic Design	**Register Number:** 20 **Name:** Gavin **Gender:** Male **Preferred subject:** Vocal Music	**Register Number:** 33 **Name:** Janice **Gender:** Female **Preferred subject:** Graphic Design	**Register Number:** 46 **Name:** Sabrina **Gender:** Female **Preferred subject:** Drawing

Register Number: 8 **Name:** Charles **Gender:** Male **Preferred subject:** Vocal Music	**Register Number:** 21 **Name:** Gilbert **Gender:** Male **Preferred subject:** Digital Music	**Register Number:** 34 **Name:** Jasmine **Gender:** Female **Preferred subject:** Drawing	**Register Number:** 47 **Name:** Taylor **Gender:** Male **Preferred subject:** Digital Music
Register Number: 9 **Name:** Debbie **Gender:** Female **Preferred subject:** Drawing	**Register Number:** 22 **Name:** Glenn **Gender:** Male **Preferred subject:** Digital Music	**Register Number:** 35 **Name:** Jill **Gender:** Female **Preferred subject:** Vocal Music	**Register Number:** 48 **Name:** Tim **Gender:** Male **Preferred subject:** Digital Music
Register Number: 10 **Name:** Dexter **Gender:** Male **Preferred subject:** Digital Music	**Register Number:** 23 **Name:** Hilda **Gender:** Female **Preferred subject:** Vocal Music	**Register Number:** 36 **Name:** Kelly **Gender:** Female **Preferred subject:** Graphic Design	**Register Number:** 49 **Name:** Tom **Gender:** Male **Preferred subject:** Graphic Design
Register Number: 11 **Name:** Elise **Gender:** Female **Preferred subject:** Vocal Music	**Register Number:** 24 **Name:** Hazel **Gender:** Female **Preferred subject:** Drawing	**Register Number:** 37 **Name:** Karen **Gender:** Female **Preferred subject:** Drawing	**Register Number:** 50 **Name:** Tammy **Gender:** Female **Preferred subject:** Vocal Music
Register Number: 12 **Name:** Edward **Gender:** Male **Preferred subject:** Graphic Design	**Register Number:** 25 **Name:** Heather **Gender:** Female **Preferred subject:** Graphic Design	**Register Number:** 38 **Name:** Kent **Gender:** Male **Preferred subject:** Digital Music	**Register Number:** 51 **Name:** Victoria **Gender:** Female **Preferred subject:** Graphic Design
Register Number: 13 **Name:** Edgar **Gender:** Male **Preferred subject:** Digital Music	**Register Number:** 26 **Name:** Hayley **Gender:** Female **Preferred subject:** Graphic Design	**Register Number:** 39 **Name:** Keith **Gender:** Male **Preferred subject:** Drawing	**Register Number:** 52 **Name:** Victor **Gender:** Male **Preferred subject:** Vocal Music

© Marshall Cavendish International (Singapore) Private Limited.

Probability

Lessons 11.1–11.4 Activity: Finding Probability

Teacher's Guide

Type of activity	Hands-on activity/game
Objective	Reinforce the skill of finding probabilities using the multiplication rule and addition rule.
Materials	• Cards on page 116 (use colored paper if possible) • Box or bag to hold the cards
Time	20–30 min
Ability levels	Mixed
Prerequisite skills	Use tree diagrams to find probabilities.
Grouping	Students should work in pairs.
Assessment of students' learning	See Lessons 11.1–11.4 Activity: Rubric.

Lessons 11.1–11.4 Activity Rubric

Category	4	3	2	1
Mathematical concepts	Explanation shows complete understanding of the mathematical concepts used to solve the problem(s).	Explanation shows substantial understanding of the mathematical concepts used to solve the problem(s).	Explanation shows some understanding of the mathematical concepts needed to solve the problem(s).	Explanation shows very limited understanding of the underlying concepts needed to solve the problem(s) OR is not written.
Reflection	The reflection shows clear thought and effort. The learning experience being reflected upon is relevant and meaningful to student and learning goals.	The reflection shows a lot of thought and effort. Student makes attempts to demonstrate relevance, but the relevance is unclear in reference to learning goals.	The reflection shows some thought and effort. Some sections of the reflection are irrelevant to student and/or learning goals.	The reflection is superficial. Most of the reflection is irrelevant to student and/or learning goals.

Lessons 11.1–11.4 Activity
Finding Probability

Step 1   Cut out the cards on page 116 and place them in a box or bag. Mix the cards well inside the box or bag.

Step 2   Decide which person will be Player 1 and which will be Player 2 throughout the activity.

Step 3   Player 1 always starts the game. Player 1 first draws a card from the box or bag. Player 2 then draws a card (*without* replacement) from the box or bag. Continue the game until one player has two cards of the same color.

Step 4   Repeat Step 3 a total of ten times. Record which player wins in each game in the table on the Student Recording Sheet.

Step 5   Answer the questions on the Student Recording Sheet.

Lessons 11.1–11.4 Activity
Student Recording Sheet

Game Number	1	2	3	4	5
Winner	Player ____	Player ____	Player ____	Player ____	Player ____

Game Number	6	7	8	9	10
Winner	Player ____	Player ____	Player ____	Player ____	Player ____

1. Who won more games?

2. Let G represent drawing a green card and R represent drawing a red card. Use this notation to list all the possible ways that Player 1 can win the game in only three turns.

3. If Player 1 draws a red card on the first turn and Player 2 then draws a red card, then the game ends with Player 1 winning the game. Why?

Reflection

4. Complete the tree diagram below and find the probability of each player winning the game. Is the game fair?

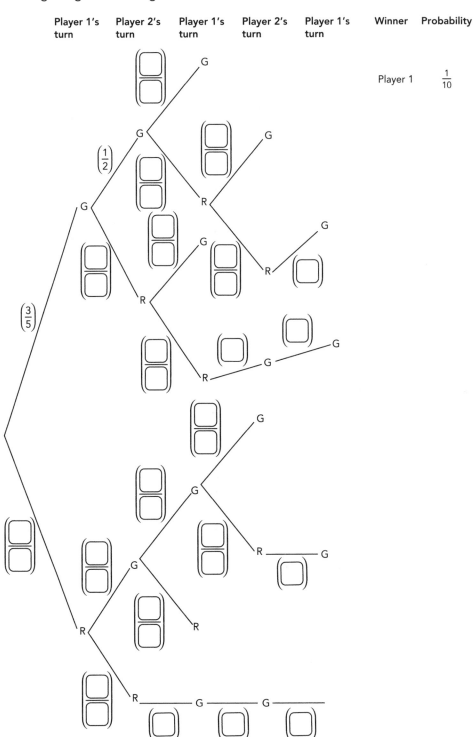

Player 1's turn	Player 2's turn	Player 1's turn	Player 2's turn	Player 1's turn	Winner	Probability

Player 1 $\frac{1}{10}$

GREEN	GREEN	GREEN

RED	RED

CHAPTER 11 Probability

Project: Using Experimental Probabilities

Teacher's Guide

Common Core Core	
Common Core State Standard	8.SP.3 Use the equation of a linear model to solve problems in the context of bivariate measurement data, interpreting the slope and intercept.
Objectives	• Explain what information the vertical intercept gives about a real-world situation. • Use the relationship between probabilities and relative frequencies.
Materials	• Graphing calculator or spreadsheet software • Ciphertext on page 122
Time	20–30 min
Ability levels	Mixed
Prerequisite skills	• Construct a scatter plot and find a line of best fit using a graphing calculator or spreadsheet software. • Find relative frequencies.
Grouping	Students should work in small groups.
Assessment of students' learning	See Chapter 11 Project: Rubric.

© Marshall Cavendish International (Singapore) Private Limited.

Chapter 11 Project
Rubric

Category	4	3	2	1
Mathematical concepts	Explanation shows complete understanding of the mathematical concepts used to solve the problem(s).	Explanation shows substantial understanding of the mathematical concepts used to solve the problem(s).	Explanation shows some understanding of the mathematical concepts needed to solve the problem(s).	Explanation shows very limited understanding of the underlying concepts needed to solve the problem(s) OR is not written.
Mathematical reasoning	Uses complex and refined logical reasoning.	Uses effective mathematical reasoning.	Shows some evidence of mathematical reasoning.	Shows little evidence of mathematical reasoning.
Neatness and organization	The work is presented in a neat, clear, organized fashion that is easy to read.	The work is presented in a neat and organized fashion that is usually easy to read.	The work is presented in an organized fashion but may be hard to read at times.	The work appears sloppy and unorganized. It is hard to know what information goes together.
Working with others	Student was an engaged partner, listening to suggestions of others and working cooperatively throughout the lesson.	Student was an engaged partner but had trouble listening to others and/or working cooperatively.	Student cooperated with others, but needed prompting to stay on task.	Student did not work effectively with others.

Chapter 11 Project
Using Experimental Probabilities

There are many ways to encode information. For example, to send a secret message, you could use a single cyclic shift on the alphabet. They could replace all 'A's with 'C's, 'B's with 'D's, …, 'Y's with 'A's, and 'Z's with 'B's. So the word 'doze' is transformed to 'fqbg'.

Changing 'doze' to 'fqbg' is called encryption. To convert 'fqbg' back into 'doze', simply reverse the system, that is, replace all 'C's with 'A's, 'D's with 'B's, and so on. The process of converting encrypted data back into its original form is called decryption. The original form of the data is called plain text, and the encrypted data is called *ciphertext*.

Look at the encrypted message on page 122. You know only that the original message is in English and that it was encrypted by performing a single cyclic shift on the alphabet. However, you do not know how far each letter was shifted. It is still possible to convert the ciphertext back into plain text by using certain patterns in the English language.

In English, some letters occur more often than others. The letter 'e' has the highest probability of occurring. In this project, you will first estimate the probability of the letter 'e' occurring in English text. Then you will convert the encrypted message.

Step 1   The table below shows how many times the letter 'E' occurs in ten randomly selected samples of English text.

Total Number of Letters (x)	100	400	500	320	200	260	330	420	150	160
Number of Times 'e' Occurs (y)	15	45	62	34	29	28	40	48	18	15

Use a graphing calculator or spreadsheet software. Enter the data in the table as two lists or in a spreadsheet. Construct a scatter plot of the data and find its corresponding line of best fit. Record the equation of the line of best fit on the Student Recording Sheet.

Step 2   Find the slope of the line, rounding your answer to the nearest hundredth.

Step 3   Find the relative frequency of each letter in the encrypted message on page 120. Record your results in the table on the Student Recording Sheet. Which letter has the greatest frequency?

Step 4   The letter from Step 3 represents 'E' in the message. Use this to complete the decryption table. Then use the table to convert the ciphertext back into plain text.

Step 5   Share with the class how you converted the encrypted message back into the original message.

Step 6   Answer the questions on the Student Recording Sheet.

Chapter 11 Project
Student Recording Sheet

1. Write the equation of line of best fit. Round the slope and the *y*-intercept to the nearest hundredth.

2. Find the slope of the line. Explain what the slope represents in terms of the data in the table.

Letter	Frequency in Ciphertext	Relative Frequency
A		
B		
C		
D		
E		
F		
G		
H		
I		
J		
K		
L		
M		
N		
O		
P		
Q		
R		
S		
T		
U		
V		
W		
X		
Y		
Z		

Decryption table

Letter	Letter After Cyclic Shift
A	
B	
C	
D	
E	
F	
G	
H	
I	
J	
K	
L	
M	
N	
O	
P	
Q	
R	
S	
T	
U	
V	
W	
X	
Y	
Z	

3. What is the original message? Explain.

Chapter 11 Project
Materials

Encrypted message:

R M G I   H E C   X S   C S Y !

A I P G S Q I   X S   Q E X L I Q E X M G W   G P Y F.

J S V   R I A   Q I Q F I V W,   Q I I X   M R   Q E X L   V S S Q

E J X I V   G P E W W.

Total number of letters in the message: 73

Solutions

Lesson 1.2 Activity (p. 4)

Shaded Part of Pattern	Number of Octagons in Shaded Part of Pattern	Number of Squares in Shaded Part of Pattern	Number of Times Pattern is Repeated	Number of Octagons in Complete Pattern	Number of Squares in Complete Pattern
	2	2	24	$2^4 \cdot 3$	$2^4 \cdot 3$

Shaded Part of Pattern	Number of Squares in Shaded Part of Pattern	Number of Equilateral Triangles in Shaded Part of Pattern	Number of Times Pattern is Repeated	Number of Squares in Complete Pattern	Number of Equilateral Triangles in Complete Pattern
	3	6	9	3^3	$2 \cdot 3^3$

Shaded Part of Pattern	Number of Squares in Shaded Part of Pattern	Number of Equilateral Triangles in Shaded Part of Pattern	Number of Times Pattern is Repeated	Number of Squares in Complete Pattern	Number of Equilateral Triangles in Complete Pattern
	4	8	12	$2^4 \cdot 3$	$2^5 \cdot 3$

1. The product of powers property

2. I can use the property when finding the product of any powers that have the same base.

3. When finding the product of two expressions with the same base, I can add their exponents and use this exponent with the same base.

Chapter 1 Project (p. 10)

Number of Rectangles
64

Portion of page	Number of Rectangles in Exponential Notation
1	2^6
$\dfrac{1}{2}$	$2^6 \div 2 = 2^{6-1} = 2^5$
$\dfrac{1}{4}$	$2^6 \div 2 \div 2 = 2^6 \div 2^2$ $= 2^{6-2} = 2^4$
$\dfrac{1}{8}$	$2^6 \div 2 \div 2 \div 2 = 2^6 \div 2^3$ $= 2^{6-3} = 2^3$
$\dfrac{1}{16}$	$2^6 \div 2 \div 2 \div 2 \div 2$ $= 2^6 \div 2^4 = 2^{6-4} = 2^2$
$\dfrac{1}{32}$	$2^6 \div 2 \div 2 \div 2 \div 2 \div 2$ $= 2^6 \div 2^5 = 2^{6-5} = 2$
$\dfrac{1}{64}$	$2^6 \div 2 \div 2 \div 2 \div 2 \div 2 \div 2$ $= 2^6 \div 2^6 = 2^{6-6} = 2^0 = 1$

1. The quotient of powers property

2. Answers vary.

3. When finding the quotient of two expressions with the same base, I can subtract the exponent of the divisor from the exponent of the dividend, and use it with the same base.

Lesson 2.2 Activity (p. 14)

Expression	$6.3 \cdot 10^{-5}$ $- 3.3 \cdot 10^{-5}$	$2.2 \cdot 10^{-2}$ $- 1.3 \cdot 10^{-3}$
Rewrite Expression	–	$22 \cdot 10^{-3}$ $- 1.3 \cdot 10^{-3}$
Use Properties of Exponents	$(6.3 - 3.3)$ $\cdot 10^{-5}$	$(22 - 1.3)$ $\cdot 10^{-3}$
Answer (in scientific notation)	$3 \cdot 10^{-5}$	$2.07 \cdot 10^{-2}$

Expression	$1.3 \cdot 10^{-3}$ $- 3.4 \cdot 10^{-4}$	$7.3 \cdot 10^{4}$ $+ 7.3 \cdot 10^{3}$
Rewrite Expression	$13 \cdot 10^{-4}$ $- 3.4 \cdot 10^{-4}$	$73 \cdot 10^{3}$ $+ 7.3 \cdot 10^{3}$
Use Properties of Exponents	$(13 - 3.4)$ $\cdot 10^{-4}$	$(73 + 7.3)$ $\cdot 10^{3}$
Answer (in scientific notation)	$9.6 \cdot 10^{-4}$	$8.03 \cdot 10^{4}$

Expression	$6 \cdot 10^{6}$ $+ 0.5 \cdot 10^{5}$	$89 \cdot 10^{5}$ $+ 3.3 \cdot 10^{6}$
Rewrite Expression	$60 \cdot 10^{5}$ $+ 0.5 \cdot 10^{5}$	$8.9 \cdot 10^{6}$ $+ 3.3 \cdot 10^{6}$
Use Properties of Exponents	$(60 + 0.5)$ $\cdot 10^{5}$	$(8.9 + 3.3)$ $\cdot 10^{6}$
Answer (in scientific notation)	$6.05 \cdot 10^{6}$	$1.22 \cdot 10^{7}$

Expression	$9.3 \cdot 10^{4}$ $- 4.1 \cdot 10^{4}$	$8.7 \cdot 10^{5}$ $- 2.1 \cdot 10^{4}$
Rewrite Expression	–	$87 \cdot 10^{4}$ $- 2.1 \cdot 10^{4}$
Use Properties of Exponents	$(9.3 - 4.1)$ $\cdot 10^{4}$	$(87 - 2.1)$ $\cdot 10^{4}$
Answer (in scientific notation)	$5.2 \cdot 10^{4}$	$8.49 \cdot 10^{5}$

Expression	$2.8 \cdot 10^{4}$ $- 3.6 \cdot 10^{3}$	$2.6 \cdot 10^{-5}$ $+ 2.6 \cdot 10^{-6}$
Rewrite Expression	$28 \cdot 10^{3}$ $- 3.6 \cdot 10^{3}$	$26 \cdot 10^{-6}$ $+ 2.6 \cdot 10^{-6}$
Use Properties of Exponents	$(28 - 3.6)$ $\cdot 10^{3}$	$(26 + 2.6)$ $\cdot 10^{-6}$
Answer (in scientific notation)	$2.44 \cdot 10^{4}$	$2.86 \cdot 10^{-5}$

Expression	$1 \cdot 10^{-4}$ $+ 0.3 \cdot 10^{-5}$	$48 \cdot 10^{-5}$ $+ 3.9 \cdot 10^{-4}$
Rewrite Expression	$10 \cdot 10^{-5}$ $+ 0.3 \cdot 10^{-5}$	$4.8 \cdot 10^{-4}$ $+ 3.9 \cdot 10^{-4}$
Use Properties of Exponents	$(10 + 0.3)$ $\cdot 10^{-5}$	$(4.8 + 3.9)$ $\cdot 10^{-4}$
Answer (in scientific notation)	$1.03 \cdot 10^{-4}$	$8.7 \cdot 10^{-4}$

Expression	$2.3 \cdot 10^3$ $+ 1.8 \cdot 10^3$	$3.3 \cdot 10^5$ $+ 2.6 \cdot 10^4$
Rewrite Expression	–	$3.3 \cdot 10^5$ $+ 0.26 \cdot 10^5$
Use Properties of Exponents	$(2.3 + 1.8)$ $\cdot 10^3$	$(3.3 + 0.26)$ $\cdot 10^5$
Answer (in scientific notation)	$4.1 \cdot 10^3$	$3.56 \cdot 10^5$

Expression	$5 \cdot 10^5$ $- 4.5 \cdot 10^4$	$74 \cdot 10^{-5}$ $- 2.4 \cdot 10^{-4}$
Rewrite Expression	$5 \cdot 10^5$ $- 0.45 \cdot 10^5$	$7.4 \cdot 10^{-4}$ $- 2.4 \cdot 10^{-4}$
Use Properties of Exponents	$(5 - 0.45)$ $\cdot 10^5$	$(7.4 - 2.4)$ $\cdot 10^{-4}$
Answer (in scientific notation)	$4.55 \cdot 10^5$	$5.0 \cdot 10^{-4}$

Expression	$4.5 \cdot 10^7$ $+ 7.6 \cdot 10^6$	$5.5 \cdot 10^{-5}$ $- 5.5 \cdot 10^{-6}$
Rewrite Expression	$4.5 \cdot 10^7$ $+ 0.76 \cdot 10^7$	$5.5 \cdot 10^{-5}$ $- 0.55 \cdot 10^{-5}$
Use Properties of Exponents	$(4.5 + 0.76)$ $\cdot 10^7$	$(5.5 - 0.55)$ $\cdot 10^{-5}$
Answer (in scientific notation)	$5.26 \cdot 10^7$	$4.95 \cdot 10^{-5}$

Expression	$53 \cdot 10^5$ $- 3.3 \cdot 10^6$	$5.4 \cdot 10^{-6}$ $+ 6.4 \cdot 10^{-6}$
Rewrite Expression	$5.3 \cdot 10^6$ $- 3.3 \cdot 10^6$	–
Use Properties of Exponents	$(5.3 - 3.3)$ $\cdot 10^6$	$(5.4 + 6.4)$ $\cdot 10^{-6}$
Answer (in scientific notation)	$2.0 \cdot 10^6$	$11.8 \cdot 10^{-6}$ $= 1.18 \cdot 10^{-5}$

Expression	$4 \cdot 10^{-4}$ $- 3.9 \cdot 10^{-5}$	$6 \cdot 10^6$ $+ 0.5 \cdot 10^5$
Rewrite Expression	$4 \cdot 10^{-4}$ $- 0.39 \cdot 10^{-4}$	$6 \cdot 10^6$ $+ 0.05 \cdot 10^6$
Use Properties of Exponents	$(4 - 0.39)$ $\cdot 10^{-4}$	$(6 + 0.05)$ $\cdot 10^6$
Answer (in scientific notation)	$3.61 \cdot 10^{-4}$	$6.05 \cdot 10^6$

Expression	$6.5 \cdot 10^{-4}$ $+ 4.2 \cdot 10^{-5}$	$3.2 \cdot 10^{-3}$ $+ 6.1 \cdot 10^{-4}$
Rewrite Expression	$6.5 \cdot 10^{-4}$ $+ 0.42 \cdot 10^{-4}$	$3.2 \cdot 10^{-3}$ $+ 0.61 \cdot 10^{-3}$
Use Properties of Exponents	$(6.5 + 0.42)$ $\cdot 10^{-4}$	$(3.2 + 0.61)$ $\cdot 10^{-3}$
Answer (in scientific notation)	$6.92 \cdot 10^{-4}$	$3.81 \cdot 10^{-3}$

Chapter 2 Project (p. 20)

Answers vary. Sample:

Expression	A · B + A · B	A · B − A · B
Numerical Expression	$5.9 \cdot 10^6$ $+ 3.4 \cdot 10^6$	$4.4 \cdot 10^4$ $- 3.7 \cdot 10^4$
Rewrite Expression	−	$44 \cdot 10^3$ $- 37 \cdot 10^3$
Prefix Form	5.9 Mm + 3.4 Mm	44 km − 37 km
Answer	9.3 Mm	7 km

Expression	A · C + A · C	A · C − A · C
Numerical Expression	$2.5 \cdot 10^{-6}$ $+ 1.6 \cdot 10^{-6}$	$3.2 \cdot 10^{-3}$ $- 1.2 \cdot 10^{-3}$
Prefix Form	2.5 µm + 1.6 µm	3.2 mm − 1.2 mm
Answer	4.1 µm	2 mm

Expression	A · B · A · B	A · C · A · C
Numerical Expression	$2.4 \cdot 10^3$ $\cdot 2.1 \cdot 10^3$	$6.2 \cdot 10^{-3}$ $\cdot 1.5 \cdot 10^{-3}$
Prefix Form	2.4 km · 2.1 km	6.2 µm · 1.5 µm
Answer	5.04 km	9.3 µm

Expression	A · B ÷ A · B	A · C ÷ A · C
Numerical Expression	$6.3 \cdot 10^6$ $\div 0.3 \cdot 10^3$	$7.2 \cdot 10^{-6}$ $\div 1.2 \cdot 10^{-3}$
Prefix Form	6.3 Mm ÷ 0.3 km	7.2 µm ÷ 1.2 mm
Answer	21 km $= 2.1 \cdot 10$ km	6 mm

1. Answers vary. Sample: Gigabytes and terabytes for measuring storage space on hard disks. Answers may vary but could involve reasons such as prefixes help us to make the very large and very small numbers more manageable.

Lesson 3.1 Activity (pp. 25–26)

1. Let x be $0.\overline{1}$.
$$10x = 1.\overline{1}$$
$$10x - x = 1.\overline{1} - 0.\overline{1}$$
$$9x = 1$$
$$\frac{9x}{9} = \frac{1}{9}$$
$$x = \frac{1}{9}$$

2. Let x be $0.\overline{2}$.
$$10x = 2.\overline{2}$$
$$10x - x = 2.\overline{2} - 0.\overline{2}$$
$$9x = 2$$
$$\frac{9x}{9} = \frac{2}{9}$$
$$x = \frac{2}{9}$$

3. Let x be $0.\overline{3}$.
$$10x = 3.\overline{3}$$
$$10x - x = 3.\overline{3} - 0.\overline{3}$$
$$9x = 3$$
$$\frac{9x}{9} = \frac{3}{9}$$
$$x = \frac{3}{9} = \frac{1}{3}$$

4. Let x be $0.\overline{4}$.

$$10x = 4.\overline{4}$$
$$10x - x = 4.\overline{4} - 0.\overline{4}$$
$$9x = 4$$
$$\frac{9x}{9} = \frac{4}{9}$$
$$x = \frac{4}{9}$$

Repeating Decimal	$0.\overline{5}$	$0.\overline{6}$	$0.\overline{7}$	$0.\overline{8}$
Fraction	$\frac{5}{9}$	$\frac{6}{9} = \frac{2}{3}$	$\frac{7}{9}$	$\frac{8}{9}$

5. Each repeating decimal has one single repeating digit, starting from the tenths place.

6. When these repeating decimals are written as fractions, the repeating digit is the numerator and the denominator is 9.

7. Let x be $0.\overline{09}$.

$$100x = 9.\overline{09}$$
$$100x - x = 9.\overline{09} - 0.\overline{09}$$
$$99x = 9$$
$$\frac{99x}{99} = \frac{9}{99}$$
$$x = \frac{1}{11}$$

8. Let x be $0.\overline{18}$.

$$100x = 18.\overline{18}$$
$$100x - x = 18.\overline{18} - 0.\overline{18}$$
$$99x = 18$$
$$\frac{99x}{99} = \frac{18}{99}$$
$$x = \frac{2}{11}$$

9. Let x be $0.\overline{27}$.

$$100x = 27.\overline{27}$$
$$100x - x = 27.\overline{27} - 0.\overline{27}$$
$$99x = 27$$
$$\frac{99x}{99} = \frac{27}{99}$$
$$x = \frac{3}{11}$$

10. Let x be $0.\overline{36}$.

$$100x = 36.\overline{36}$$
$$100x - x = 36.\overline{36} - 0.\overline{36}$$
$$99x = 36$$
$$\frac{99x}{99} = \frac{36}{99}$$
$$x = \frac{4}{11}$$

Repeating Decimal	$0.\overline{45}$	$0.\overline{54}$	$0.\overline{63}$
Fraction	$\frac{5}{11}$	$\frac{6}{11}$	$\frac{7}{11}$

Repeating Decimal	$0.\overline{72}$	$0.\overline{81}$	$0.\overline{90}$
Fraction	$\frac{8}{11}$	$\frac{9}{11}$	$\frac{10}{11}$

11. Each repeating decimal has two repeating digits which form a multiple of 9.

12. When these repeating decimals are written as fractions, the numerator is the number of 9's there are in the repeating digits and the denominator is 11.

Chapter 3 Project (p. 30)

Let x be the total cost for Mr. Wheel's Rentals.
Let y be the total cost for Grand Auto Rentals.
Let m be the distance traveled.
Mr. Wheel's Rentals: $x = 90 + 0.10m$
Grand Auto Rentals: $y = 75 + 0.15m$

1. Substitute $m = 100$ in each equation.
$$x = 90 + 0.10(100)$$
$$= 90 + 10$$
$$= 100$$
Mr. Wheel's Rentals charges $100 for 100 miles.
$$y = 75 + 0.15(100)$$
$$= 75 + 15$$
$$= 90$$
Grand Auto Rentals charges $90 for 100 miles.
Claudia should choose Grand Auto Rentals.

2.

$$90 + 0.10m = 75 + 0.15m$$
$$90 + 0.10m - 0.10m = 75 + 0.15m - 0.10m$$
$$90 = 75 + 0.05m$$
$$90 - 75 = 75 + 0.05m - 75$$
$$15 = 0.05m$$
$$\frac{15}{0.05} = \frac{0.05m}{0.05}$$
$$m = 300$$

If Claudia drives 300 miles, the cost is the same at both companies.

3. Substitute $x = 130$ into the equation for Mr. Wheel's Rentals.

$$130 = 90 + 0.10m$$
$$130 - 90 = 90 + 0.10m - 90$$
$$40 = 0.10m$$
$$m = 400$$

Claudia can travel 400 miles if she rents from Mr. Wheel's Rentals with a budget of $130.
Substitute $y = 130$ into the equation for Grand Auto Rentals.

$$130 = 75 + 0.15m$$
$$130 - 75 = 75 + 0.15m - 75$$
$$55 = 0.15m$$
$$\frac{55}{0.15} = \frac{0.15m}{0.15}$$
$$m \approx 366.7$$

Claudia can travel about 366.7 miles if she rents from Grand Auto Rentals with a budget of $130.
Claudia should choose Mr. Wheel's Rentals.

Lesson 4.3 Activity (p. 34)

$y = mx + b$	Slope, m	y-intercept, b
$y = -3x + \frac{7}{2}$	-3	$\frac{7}{2}$
$y = 3x - 8$	3	-8
$y = -\frac{3}{8}x + \frac{5}{8}$	$-\frac{3}{8}$	$\frac{5}{8}$
$y = \frac{2}{5}x + \frac{6}{5}$	$\frac{2}{5}$	$\frac{6}{5}$
$y = \frac{1}{4}x + \frac{9}{4}$	$\frac{1}{4}$	$\frac{9}{4}$
$y = 2$	0	2
$y = -x - 1$	-1	-1
$y = -\frac{5}{7}x + 5$	$-\frac{5}{7}$	5
$y = -\frac{4}{9}x + 4$	$-\frac{4}{9}$	4
$y = -\frac{1}{4}x + \frac{13}{4}$	$-\frac{1}{4}$	$\frac{13}{4}$
$y = 2x + 5$	2	5
$y = \frac{1}{3}x + \frac{1}{2}$	$\frac{1}{3}$	$\frac{1}{2}$
$y = -4x - 2$	-4	-2
$y = -\frac{1}{4}x - \frac{1}{2}$	$-\frac{1}{4}$	$-\frac{1}{2}$
$y = -3x + \frac{2}{5}$	-3	$\frac{2}{5}$
$y = -x + 2$	-1	2
$y = 3x - 16$	3	-16
$y = -3x + 27$	-3	27
$y = \frac{1}{2}x + 5$	$\frac{1}{2}$	5
$y = -\frac{1}{4}x + 9$	$-\frac{1}{4}$	9

1. Answers vary, but may include any of the following choices:
   - given the equation in non-slope-intercept form,
   - given the slope and *y*-intercept,
   - given the slope and a point on the line,
   - given two points.

2. Answers vary, but may include any of the following choices:
   - given the equation in non-slope-intercept form,
   - given the slope and *y*-intercept,
   - given the slope and a point on the line,
   - given two points.

3. Example: Rewriting linear equations in slope-intercept form allows me to identify the slope, *m*, and *y*-intercept, *b*, easily.

Lesson 4.4 Activity (pp. 40–42)

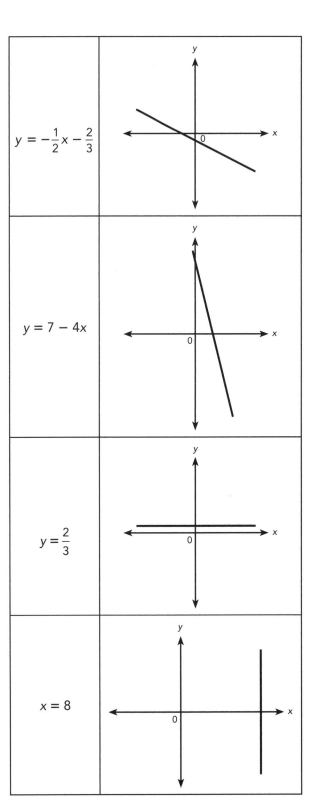

Equation	Graph
$y = \frac{3}{4}x + 1$	
$y = 5x - 2$	
$y = -\frac{1}{2}x - \frac{2}{3}$	
$y = 7 - 4x$	
$y = \frac{2}{3}$	
$x = 8$	

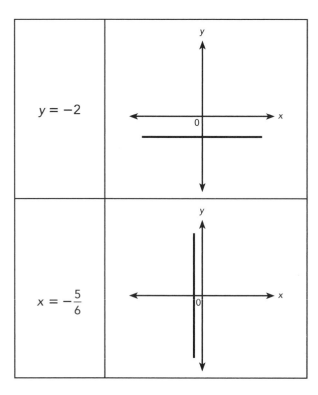

| $y = -2$ | (graph: horizontal line below x-axis) |
| $x = -\dfrac{5}{6}$ | (graph: vertical line left of y-axis) |

1. $y = \dfrac{3}{4}x + 1$ and $y = 5x - 2$. Both graphs go up from left to right.

2. $y = -\dfrac{1}{2}x - \dfrac{2}{3}$ and $y = 7 - 4x$. Both graphs go down from left to right.

3. $x = 8$ and $x = -\dfrac{5}{6}$. Yes; Press (2ND) (PRGM) to select 4: Vertical. To graph $x = 8$, press 8 and (ENTER). The x-coordinates of any two points on the line are the same.

4. $y = \dfrac{2}{3}$ and $y = -2$. The y-coordinates of any two points on the line are the same.

5. The direction a line slopes and how steep the line is are both determined by the value of a line's slope.

Chapter 4 Project (p. 46)

Answers vary, depending on the students' choice of method of exercise and rate of exercise.

1. The ratios are all the same.

2. The ratios are equal, and are the same as the ones found in Question 1.

3. The slope of the line is the same as the ratio $\dfrac{y}{x}$. It is the same as the ratio of the lengths of the sides of the right triangles, and it is equal to the rate of exercise each student used.

4. The graph would shift up 1 unit, but the slope would stay the same as the ratio of the lengths of the sides of the new right triangles remain the same.

Lesson 5.2 Activity (p. 50)

System of Equations	Player 1 (Elimination Method) Equation 1 in ready-to-combine Form	Player 2 (Substitution Method) Equation 1 in ready-to-substitute Form
$x + y = 8$ $2x + y = 11$	$2x + 2y = 16$	$x = 8 - y$
$3x + y = 9$ $2y - 3x = 5$	$6x + 2y = 18$	$3x = 9 - y$
$x + y = 7$ $x + 2y = 12$	$2x + 2y = 14$	$x = 7 - y$
$x + y = 6$ $3x - y = 2$	$3x + 3y = 18$	$y = 6 - x$
$2x + y = 7$ $2y - 2x = 2$	$4x + 2y = 14$	$2x = 7 - y$
$x + 2y = 9$ $2x + 2y = 10$	$2x + 4y = 18$	$2y = 9 - x$

1. Answers vary.

2. Yes, but only for substitution method. Answers vary. Sample: $y = 8 - x$.

3. Answers vary. For the elimination method, if both unknowns of the equations have different coefficients, one equation should be multiplied by a constant to achieve the same coefficient as the other equation. For the substitution method, there is no need to simplify if the unknown has the same coefficient as the other equation.

Chapter 5 Project (p. 56)

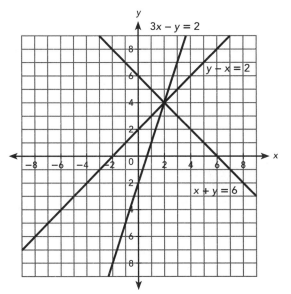

1. $x + y = 6$ — Equation 1
$3x - y = 2$ — Equation 2
Solution: Use elimination method
Add Equations 1 and 2:
$4x = 8$
$x = 2$
Substitute $x = 2$ into Equation 2:
$3(2) - y = 2$
$y = 4$
Yes, this answer corresponds to the intersection point on the graph.

2. Answers vary. Sample equation:
$y - x = 2$. The answer is the same as the previous answer because all three lines intersect at the same point.

3. Answers vary. The equation should have the same slope as any of the three lines in the graph.

4. Answers vary. Two of the equations should have the same slope and y-intercept.

5. Answers vary.

Lesson 6.2 Activity (p. 60)

Answers vary, based on the availability of a thermometer and objects to measure.

Object	Temperature (°C)	Temperature (°F)
Boiling water	100	212
Ice cube	0	32
Normal human body temperature	37	98.6
Room temperature	20	68
Chilled orange juice	13.9	57

1. Answers vary. Samples: The difference between two degrees Celsius is greater than the difference between two degrees Fahrenheit; the zeroes are in different places on the two different scales.

2. Answers vary. Sample:

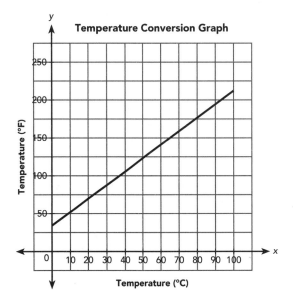

3. Answers vary. Sample: $f(C) = 1.8C + 32$

4. The slope, 1.8, represents the ratio of the size of one degree Celsius to one degree Fahrenheit. A change in temperature gives a larger difference in degrees Fahrenheit than degrees Celsius. The *y*-intercept, 32, means that 0°C is equivalent to 32°F.

Chapter 6 Project (p. 66)

Sample:

Graph	Type of Slope(s)	Description
A	Positive, zero	The person travels away from home, then stays in one place.
B	Positive	The person travels away from home.
C	Positive, zero, positive	The person travels away from home, stays in one place, then travels further away from home.
D	Negative	The person starts out away from home, and travels until he is home.
E	Negative, zero, positive	The person starts out away from home, stays in one place for a time, then travels away from home.
F	Positive, negative, positive, negative	The person starts at home, travels away, returns home, travels away, and returns home again.

1. Graphs B and D have constant rates of change. This means that the person is traveling at a steady rate and always either approaching home or traveling away from home.

2. The person is traveling away from home.

3. The person is traveling home.

4. The person stays in one place.

5. Answers vary. Sample:

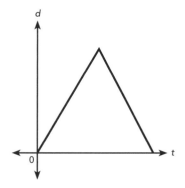

The section with the positive slope represents traveling away from home, and the section with the negative slope represents traveling home.

Lesson 7.1 Activity (p. 70)

1.

Right Triangle	Length of Vertical Leg (cm)	Length of Horizontal Leg (cm)	Length of Hypotenuse (cm)
A	6	2	$\sqrt{6^2 + 2^2} = \sqrt{40}$
B	5	5	$\sqrt{5^2 + 5^2} = \sqrt{50}$
C	9	3	$\sqrt{9^2 + 3^2} = \sqrt{90}$

2.

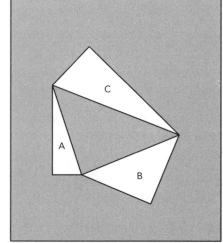

The triangle enclosed has sides of lengths $\sqrt{40}$, $\sqrt{50}$, and $\sqrt{90}$ centimeters. $\left(\sqrt{40}\right)^2 + \left(\sqrt{50}\right)^2 = \left(\sqrt{90}\right)^2$. So, by the converse of the Pythagorean Theorem, the enclosed triangle is a right triangle.

3. Use one of the corners of the paper as a right angle. Label the right angle as $\angle PQR$. Use a ruler to measure the length of $\overline{PQ}$ to be 8 centimeters and the length of $\overline{QR}$ to be 4 centimeters along the sides of the paper. By Pythagorean Theorem, $PR = \sqrt{8^2 + 4^2} = \sqrt{80}$.

Chapter 7 Project (p. 74)

1. 1) Leave the house to buy medicine from the pharmacy.
   2) Have breakfast at Gourmet Inn.
   3) Take clothing to the dry cleaner.
   4) Buy vegetables and fruits at the supermarket.
   5) Return home.

2. Distance from house to pharmacy
   $= \sqrt{(2-1)^2 + [3-(-1)]^2}$
   $= \sqrt{1^2 + 4^2}$
   $= \sqrt{17}$ units

   Distance from pharmacy to Gourmet Inn
   $= \sqrt{[1-(-2)]^2 + [(-1)-1]^2}$
   $= \sqrt{3^2 + (-2)^2}$
   $= \sqrt{13}$ units

   Distance from Gourmet Inn to dry cleaner
   $= \sqrt{[-1-(-2)]^2 + (5-1)^2}$
   $= \sqrt{1^2 + 4^2}$
   $= \sqrt{17}$ units

   Distance from dry cleaner to supermarket
   $= |6-5|$
   $= 1$ unit

   Distance from supermarket to house
   $= \sqrt{(-1-2)^2 + (6-3)^2}$
   $= \sqrt{(-3)^2 + 3^2}$
   $= \sqrt{18}$ units

Total distance
$= \left(\sqrt{17} + \sqrt{13} + \sqrt{17} + 1 + \sqrt{18}\right) \times 100\,\text{m}$
$\approx 1709.4\,\text{m}$

3. The last item on the itinerary is buying vegetables and fruits, so Mrs. Smith doesn't have to carry the groceries throughout the trip.

Lessons 8.1–8.3 Activity (p. 78)

Task A
Picture I

Picture II

Object Number	Type of Geometric Transformation
1	Translation
2	90° clockwise/counterclockwise rotation
3	Reflection
4	180° rotation (or half turn)
5	90° clockwise/counterclockwise rotation
6	Reflection

Task B

Word: REWARD

Task C

Wrong Image	Correct Image
HT	TH
ZT	ƧT
MP	Mᒬ

1. Answers vary.

2. Answers vary.

3. Answers vary.

Lesson 8.3 Activity (p. 86)

Letters/Numbers	Images
A	∀
B	ᗺ
H	H
X	X
5	Ƨ
6	9
7	ㄥ
8	8
9	6

Original product code: H689I

1. The letters are in descending (instead of ascending) order.

2. Only H, I, 6, 8, 9 from the lists are still readable symbols when turned upside. Since the letters and numbers of a legitimate product code are distinct and in ascending order, the only possible choice is H689I.

3. 180° rotation

Chapter 8 Project (p. 90)
Answers vary. Examples are given.

Shape A
Translate parallelogram A 7 units to the right and 2 units down.

Shape B
Reflect parallelogram B in the y-axis to obtain image parallelogram B'. Translate parallelogram B' 7 units to the right.

Shape C
Rotate rectangle C 90° clockwise about the origin to obtain image rectangle C'. Translate rectangle C' 4 units to the right.

Shape D

Dilate square D with center at the origin and scale factor 2 to obtain image square D'. Translate square D' 6 units to the right and 11 units up.

Shape E

Translate parallelogram E 6 units to the right and 5 units up.

Shape F

Reflect parallelogram F in the x-axis.

Lesson 9.2 Activity (p. 96)

1–3. Answers vary, based on the scale factors chosen, but students should notice that the ratio of the areas of the similar figures is the square of the scale factor for the similar figures.

4. Answers vary. Sample: If the scale factor of two similar polygons is s, then ratio of their areas is s^2. This is because to find an area, you multiply two measures, such as base and height. If the base and the height are both multiplied by s, then the area is multiplied by s^2.

Chapter 9 Project (p. 100)

Vertical Line	Horizontal Line	Coordinates of A″	Coordinates of B″
$x = 1$	$y = 1$	$(-1, -4)$	$(-1, -2)$
$x = 0$	$y = 0$	$(-3, -6)$	$(-3, -4)$
$x = 2$	$y = 3$	$(1, 0)$	$(1, 2)$
$x = -2$	$y = -1$	$(-7, -8)$	$(-7, -6)$

Vertical Line	Horizontal Line	Coordinates of C″	Center of Rotation
$x = 1$	$y = 1$	$(-4, -2)$	$(1, 1)$
$x = 0$	$y = 0$	$(-6, -4)$	$(0, 0)$
$x = 2$	$y = 3$	$(-2, 2)$	$(2, 3)$
$x = -2$	$y = -1$	$(-10, -6)$	$(-2, -1)$

1. Answers vary. Sample: The side lengths and the angle measures of the triangles stay the same when they are reflected, so $\triangle ABC'' \cong \triangle A'B'C'$.

2. The x-coordinate of the center of rotation coincides with the equation of the vertical line of reflection. The y-coordinate of the center of rotation coincides with the equation of the horizontal line of reflection.

3. Reflecting a figure in a vertical line $x = a$ and then in a horizontal line $y = b$ is equivalent to a 180° rotation of the figure about (a, b).

4. No, the image triangle is the same regardless of the order.

Lessons 10.1–10.2 Activity (p. 104)

Answers vary, depending on the students' foot lengths and heights.

1. The scatter plot indicates a strong and positive linear association.

2. An example of an invalid conclusion may occur when $x = 0$, i.e. when the foot length is zero.

3. Answers vary, depending on the equation of line of best fit obtained. Sample:
- The scatter plot shows a strong and positive linear association between the two sets of quantitative data. If $x = 24$ lies within the data range, the estimated value is reliable.

- The scatter plot shows a strong and positive linear association between the two sets of quantitative data. If $x = 24$ lies outside the data range, the estimated value is not reliable. This is because the linear model may not be valid in the case of extrapolation.

4. The equation of a line of best fit can sometimes be used to make estimates or predictions.

Chapter 10 Project (p. 108)

1. The simple random sampling method is used. Every member of a population has an equal chance of being selected for the sample. In other words, members are selected from a population without any pre-planned order.

2. Answers vary. Sample:

Preferred Class

Gender		Drawing	Graphic Design	Vocal Music	Digital Music	Total
	Female	3	4	1	1	9
	Male	1	1	4	5	11
	Total	4	5	5	6	20

3. Answers vary. Sample:

Preferred Class

Gender		Drawing	Graphic Design	Vocal Music	Digital Music	Total
	Female	$\frac{1}{3}$	$\frac{4}{9}$	$\frac{1}{9}$	$\frac{1}{9}$	1
	Male	$\frac{1}{11}$	$\frac{1}{11}$	$\frac{4}{11}$	$\frac{5}{11}$	1

4. It appears that females prefer Graphic Design and Drawing while males prefer Digital Music and Vocal Music.

5. No, the suggestion is not valid. There may be a group of students who are selected for both random samples.

Lessons 11.1–11.4 Activity (pp. 114–115)

1. Answers vary, depending on the color of the cards drawn by the players.

2. (G, G, G); (G, R, G); (R, G, R)

3. If both red cards are drawn by different players, then only green cards can be drawn. Player 1 will draw a green card, Player 2 will draw a green card, then Player 1 will draw a green card.

Reflection

4.

P(Player 1 wins)
= P(G, G, G) + P(G, G, R, R, G) + P(G, R, G) + P(G, R, R, G, G) + P(R, G, G, R, G) + P(R, G, R) + P(R, R, G, G, G)
= 0.1 + 0.1 + 0.2 + 0.1 + 0.1 + 0.1 + 0.1
= 0.8
P(Player 2 wins) = P(G, G, R, G) + P(R, G, G, G)
= 0.1 + 0.1 = 0.2
Since Player 1 has a higher probability of winning, the game is biased.

Chapter 11 Project (pp. 120–121)

1. $y \approx 0.12x + 0.69$

2. Slope ≈ 0.12
   The slope is the average of the relative frequencies of the occurrences of the letter E in the passages. It also gives the (experimental) probability of 'E' occurring in an English passage.

Letter	Frequency in Ciphertext	Relative Frequency
A	2	0.03
B	0	0
C	2	0.03
D	0	0
E	6	0.08
F	2	0.03
G	5	0.07
H	1	0.01
I	10	0.14
J	2	0.03
K	0	0
L	2	0.03
M	3	0.04
N	0	0
O	0	0
P	3	0.04
Q	8	0.11
R	3	0.04
S	7	0.10
T	0	0
U	0	0
V	4	0.05
W	4	0.05
X	7	0.10
Y	2	0.03
Z	0	0

Decryption table

Letter	Letter After Cyclic Shift
A	W
B	X
C	Y
D	Z
E	A
F	B
G	C
H	D
I	E
J	F
K	G
L	H
M	I
N	J
O	K
P	L
Q	M
R	N
S	O
T	P
U	Q
V	R
W	S
X	T
Y	U
Z	V

3. Original message:
   NICE DAY TO YOU!

   WELCOME TO MATHEMATICS CLUB.

   FOR NEW MEMBERS, MEET IN MATH ROOM AFTER CLASS.

   The relative frequency of the letter 'I' occurring in the encrypted message is the highest and is close to 0.12. So, you can guess that the letter 'I' is encrypted from the letter 'E'. Since the encryption is done using a cyclic shift on the alphabet, you can perform the same shift on each letter and obtain the decryption table. Then, use the decryption table to find the original message.

BLANK